Historical Memories of

American Saddlebred Visionaries

History and Leadership

By

Chas. L. Cook, Jr.

Copyright 2015

ISBN No. 978-1-935538-09-7

First Edition

Cover: "Highland Denmark" by George Ford Morris

With appreciation, the writer gratefully acknowledges that permission to use a reproduction of this painting has been granted by Cynthia Byers, owner of the painting and owner also of the 2014 Three-Gaited World's Champion 15.2 & Under *Don O'Neill*.

Dedicated To My Sister

Mildred Louise Cook Wuest

1915-2010

"She was always there for me."

"Points of Interest"

"Points of Interest"

"Points of Interest"

"Points of Interest"

Page

"Points of Interest"

"Points of Interest"

Historical Memories of

American Saddlebred Visionaries

Influential sire Gaines Denmark

General John Breckenridge Castleman 1841-1918 was elected President of The National Saddle Horse Breeders' Association on April 7, 1891 by leading members of saddle horse owners. The meeting took place in the office of the Farmers Home Journal, Louisville, KY when it was initiated by its editor Col. Ion B. Nall.

On April 7, 1899, the name of the organization was changed to The American Saddle Horse Breeders' Association, at an annual meeting of the stockholders. The purpose of the organization was to improve and protect the American Saddle Horse; to encourage a better breeding practice; more careful selection of both stallions and mares; and to promote adherence to a recognized type.

Gen. Castleman brought prominence as the son of David Castleman and Mary Ann Breckenridge who owned the thoroughbred and standard bred Castleton Farm at Lexington, KY. In Castleman's ancestry was his great-uncle, John Breckenridge, who served as Attorney General in Thomas Jefferson's administration and his cousin, John C. Breckenridge, Vice-President of the United States under James Buchanan.

John B. Castleman left the study of law at Transylvania University and joined the daring and exciting guerrilla fighter, Brigadier General John Hunt Morgan, and became a dashing Confederate Calvary officer in the Civil War. It was in these escapades that he recognized the Saddlebred horse capable of outlasting other horses, and he saw it maintain its noble stature under tremendous stress.

John B. Castleman

After the Civil War, he began making regular show ring appearances and occasionally judged shows. He had an imposing figure, standing six-foot three and weighing 200 pounds; either riding or judging, he was an impressive sight. His saddle-mare, Emily, took first prize at the World's Fair in 1893 and created a sensation at Madison Square Garden a little later. With the aid of the Louisville Horse Show Association, Castleman was also responsible for beginning a large show in Louisville in 1900 which was discontinued after the Association disbanded in 1908. However, the tradition of the big show in Louisville continues to this day with the Kentucky State Fair World's Championships.

Under the guidance of Castleman the collecting, recording and preserving the pedigrees of Saddle Horses began with a registry. Volume I of "The Register of the American Saddle Horse Breeders' Association" was published in **1892** by Secretary I. B. Nall. Initially seventeen stallions were designated foundation sires.

Although the original list of foundation sires contained seventeen stallions, this list was gradually reduced, and at a meeting of the association on **April 10, 1908, it was decided to list Denmark, by Imported Hedgeford, as the sole Foundation Sire.** The others on earlier lists were given numbers and placed on the Noted Deceased Sire List. The designation of Denmark alone as the Foundation Sire was made because in number of registered descendants no other sire could compare with him.

Those named to the original list of Foundation Stock, with additions and eliminations were: Brinker's Drennon, Sam Brooker, John Dillard, Tom Hall, Coleman's Eureka, Van Meter's Waxy, Cabell's Lexington, Copperbottom, Stump the Dealer, Texas, Prince Albert, Peters' Halcorn, Varnon's Roebuck, Davy Crockett), (added to the list in1893), Harrison Chief (added in 1898), and Pat Cleburne (added in 1899).

Denmark, a brown horse foaled in 1839, was a Thoroughbred. Almost all registered ASBs trace to Denmark. When bred to the fine Cockspur pacing mare known as the Stevenson mare to Denmark, he sired **Gaines Denmark** and established the Denmark family of Saddlebreds. Denmark was named the single foundation sire because more than 60 percent of the horses in the first three volumes of the registry were directly traced by male line to him. Gaines Denmark 61 was a black horse with two hind white socks and generally conceded to be the real progenitor of the American Saddlebred breed. A beautiful black stallion, he was one of the greatest show horses of his day and served in the Civil War in General Morgan's command. His contributions to the development of the breed are without rival.

Gaines Denmark was made famous by his four sons that he produced prior to his entry in the Civil War. He produced little after his return. These were Washington Denmark 64, Diamond Denmark 68, Star Denmark 71 and Sumpter Denmark 65.

The American Saddlebred has an elegant long neck that comes high out of its sloping shoulder. It is flat over its croup and has a high tail set. Most American Saddlebreds stand 15 to 16 hands tall and are of solid coat colors, such as black, brown, bay, gray, or chestnut. The Saddlebred's travel is exemplified by extreme animation and style.

In mid-1985, a committee was formed to oversee the establishment of the new American Saddle Horse Museum in the Kentucky Horse Park in Lexington. The various members had searched through old records in an effort to find any pictures of the horses which were considered to be the backbone of today's Saddlebred. Unfortunately, almost no images could be found. As an equine artist who spent many years studying Saddlebred history, James Walls was given the task of creating believable portraits of the sires as they may have appeared.

"American Saddlebred Foundation Sires"

Historical Stallion Portraits

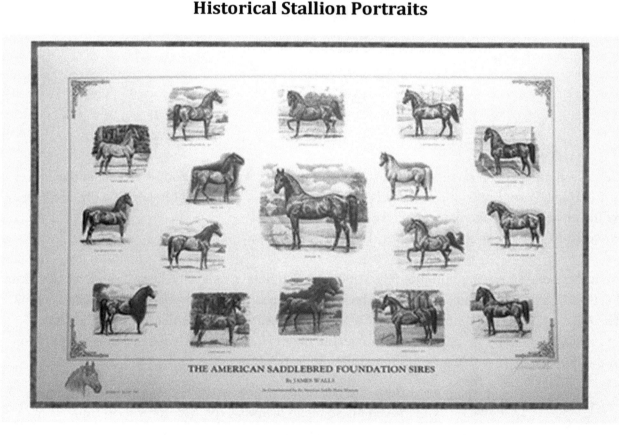

THE AMERICAN SADDLEBRED FOUNDATION SIRES
By JAMES WALLS

Denmark had been recognized as the sole "Foundation Sire," and his portrait is set in the center of the print at his rightful place. In **1991**, a year after this print was produced, the committee determined that Harrison Chief should also be considered a "Foundation Sire," and was given the title **"Harrison Chief FS".** It should be noted that Harrison Chief is shown directly to the right of Denmark FS on the finished print. Authorities have pronounced this print as an important part of Saddlebred history, this is a one-of-a-kind piece of Saddlebred history.

STATUE OF GENERAL JOHN BRECKINRIDGE CASTLEMAN

Gen. Castleman sits in civilian dress astride Carolina, his American Saddle Horse, at the entrance of Cherokee Park, Louisville, KY. This 15-foot high bonze monument honors his life and legacy by the citizens of Louisville and his friends.
Photo from *The Horse America Made*, Louis Taylor, 1944.

None has done so much to promote the American Saddlebred as has General John Breckenridge Castleman. Almost single-handedly, he brought the breed to international attention and acclaim. The National Horseman's prestigious "Castleman Award" is named after General Castleman and is given annually to individuals who devote their efforts to the advancement and promotion of the breed.

Tom Bass, the legendary negro saddle horse trainer of Mexico, MO moved his stable to Kansas City, MO for a short time. Tom Bass was on the Board of Advisors for the Kansas City Fire Department. When the Board was discussing how to raise money, **Tom suggested a horse show.**

Therefore in **1892**. the first big Kansas City horse show was held in a tent. Thus was the start of one of the biggest horse shows in the nation, the **American Royal**.

Tom was born Jan. 5, 1859 to a slave girl and her owner, William Hayden Bass. He became a world famous rider and trainer of fine saddle horses. He competed in a white man's sport and the only African-American to show horses in Madison Square Garden. He was ahead of his time in breaking race barriers. The guests in his stable at Mexico, MO included presidents and dignitaries. He **invented the "Bass bit,"** a horse bit that prevented the abuse of horses during training. His popularity attributed to making Mexico, Missouri, the original "Saddle Horse Capital of the World."

National Horse Show

Vanderbilt's Support Society and Sports Event

William K. Vanderbilt I was affluent sportsmen in **1883** at York, NY. He was a Director Nephew, Alfred G. Vanderbilt oldest indoor horse show and horse show in America. It had holders and officials. In a gesture invited 3,000 orphaned children one of the founders by a group of Madison Square Garden, New and Honorary Vice President. His was President 1909-1914. It is the one time was the most important a white tie dress code for box of charity, the Vanderbilt family in 1913 to sit in the balconies.

The National Horse Show includes international team jumping, competition for national hunters and jumpers, saddle seat equitation, American Saddlebred Division and Hackney Division. The facilities changed many times. After 1999, Saddlebred performance classes disappeared from the show.

In **2011**, on the heels of their sponsorship of the World Equestrian Games, Kentucky-based bioscience company Alltech brought the show and its legacy to their own backyard. The newly branded **Alltech National Horse Show** (ANHS) is in its new home in the prestigious Kentucky Horse Park's indoor Alltech Arena. Lexington, KY.

The American Saddlebred Division was added in 2012, with the Hackney Division added in 2013. The Alltech National Horse Show added the divisions in an effort to maintain the rich tradition of the horse show in its new home in Kentucky, a hub for some of the finest American Saddlebreds and Hackney Ponies in the country. In 2013, the combined event pairing American Saddlebred riders with hunter/jumper riders switching disciplines was well-received and very popular.

Unfortunately, due to the **light participation of entries** in the divisions over two years, the Board of Directors of the National Horse Show Association made a difficult business decision to **cancel the divisions for the 2014 Alltech National Horse Show.** Saddlebred owners need to agree to bring this horse show back to its prominence.

Madison Square Garden 1910

Alltech Arena 2011

J. W. Waring founded **"The Official Horse Show Blue Book"** in **1906** at the age of 50. He published it successfully for 29 years until his death. The Blue Book was the **show horse bible**. It was a chronicle of horse show history, with detailed show results and filled with page after page of vintage photos, many never published elsewhere. J. H. Ransom said, "That he had the pleasure and honor of working with Mr. Waring during the last years. His generosity, guidance and vision helped me

over the rough spots during the depression and enabled me to begin publishing on my own. It was the most beautiful book published for horsemen. He was one of the most clever and polished salesmen of all time. The friend of millionaires and sportsmen and horsemen, the most popular and gifted publisher of books for horsemen." This writer proudly displays the cover of the twenty-first annual edition with the outstanding three-gaited saddle horse of 1927, the gold mare Jonquil ridden by my father Charlie Cook.

Hon. Mat S. Cohen

Hon. Mat. S. Cohen was elected Commissioner of Agriculture of Kentucky, which automatically made him **President of the Kentucky State Fair Board**. Susanne (Emily Ellen Scharf) writes, "Saddle horse history contains the name of no other exactly comparable to Madison Sandidge Cohen. He was unique in individuality and versaile in accomplishments, but **a horseman, first and last** – seemingly ever since he was in swaddling clothes; a wonderful rider, a highly talented trainer, the greatest 'ring general' that ever confused a judge, such a man was 'Marvelous Mat'."

During his term of office, "Jumps" Cauthron of Missouri, presented to Mat the outline for a four-divison grand championship stake to carry a value of $10,000, a plan he had presented to, and had been turned down by the Missouri State Fair Board. Mat Cohen recognized the incalculable value of such a stake to the saddle horse breed and in the face of countless and seemingly insurmountable obstacles, **he inaugurated the $10,000 stake for five-gaited horses at the Kentucky State Fair in 1917**, which has done more to promote the breeding of the saddle horse than any other move made for the advancement of the most beautiful horse in the world.

The significance of this event is not solely on account of its representing the largest money prize that had ever been arranged for distribution for saddle horses but it would attract a list of entries that had never before been equaled in a saddle horse event. This was an event of national importance and would put the spotlight on saddle horses; thousands of people will become interested in saddle horses.

Later, Mat Cohen became manager of the Los Angeles National Horse Show and he originated the use of the loud speaker for announcing a horse show, and although as manager of the show, yet also announced the show, and no one has approached the real job of announcing that he did at this show. In 1934 he returned to Kentucky, climaxing his career as owner and publisher of the *American Horseman* which he made the outstanding publication devoted to the interests of the show horse and the horse shows.

Hon. Claude M. Thomas succeeded Castleman as President in **1918** and he was one of the founders of the American Saddle Horse Breeders' Association. He was a graduate of Princeton University and the law department of Columbia University. In 1887 he was elected to serve as Senator in the Kentucky legislature. In 1893 he was appointed by President Cleveland as United States Consul at Marseilles, France. Senator Thomas made a specialty of raising short-horn cattle and saddle horses on his farm in Bourbon County.

He was one of the organizers of the First National Bank of Paris, in 1902, and served as its President. He was President of Baldwin Packing Company of Paris and was influential in the organization of the Burley Tobacco Society.

Col. I. Beverly Nall
Secretary
1891-1912

Roger L. Lillard
Secretary
1913-1932

Charles J. Cronan, Jr.
Secretary 1932 - 1979
Executive Vice President 1979 - 1983

Charles J. Cronan, Jr. founded the first **American Saddlebred futurity program** in **1927** at the Kentucky State Fair, which is now known as the ASR Kentucky Futurity. He paid $1,160 out of his own pocket to get the futurity started. Cronan's model of futurities is the foundation for more than 28 American Saddlebred programs across the country. A futurity is a prize program for young horses, which awards purses made up of entry fees paid over a period of time by participants. Futurities are held to encourage the breeding and showing of American Saddlebred horses. Showing a foal in a futurity enhances his value and increases his earning potential. The value of the sire and dam may also be enhanced through the success of their progeny shown in futurities. The ASR Kentucky Futurity holds three divisions each year: (1) Weanling In hand, (2) Yearling In Hand and (3)Two-Year-Old Fine Harness. The divisions are open to the offspring of stallions and mares nominated to the ASR Kentucky Futurity. The classes are held at the Kentucky State Fair World's Championship Horse Show each August and are conducted under the rules of the U. S. Equestrian Federation. Cronan was a founding member of the Rock Creek Riding Club, Louisville, KY, in **1929.**

C. J. Cronan was a graduate of the Jefferson School of Law (now part of the University of Louisville) and was admitted to the Kentucky bar in 1917. Cronan was in the 138th Field Artillery of the Kentucky National Guard during World War I and had active service in World War II, attaining the rank of Colonel.

In **1932** Charles J. Cronan, Jr. became Secretary of the American Saddle Horse Breeders' Association. Intricate record keeping assured that when a certificate of registration of any Saddlebred horse is issued, the breeding, age, and identity are exactly as represented. The Directors had rules that were exacting and the office experience proved that this was all warranted. In **1949** the Association was forced to give up its old quarters in the Urban Building and found it advisable to purchase an old colonial residence at 929 South Fourth Street.

Urban Building, 122 S. Fourth St., Louisville, KY

Ann Thompson, up
Spelling Bee

Cronan brought into the office operation Miss Ann Thompson, daughter of saddle horse breeder S. J. Thompson, Knob Creek Stock Farm, Hodgenville, KY and sister of Jack Thompson who had a World Fine Harness Championship with Noble Kalarama. Her title was Office Manager and she maintained the registrations almost singlehandedly. She was intent on having the details of registration and transfer recorded correctly and as promptly as possible.

In a report by Cronan to the Association in **1949**, he said that twenty-five years ago the registrations varied from 500-800 horses per year. During 1948 we registered 4,477 and that these registrations came from every state and three foreign countries. The number of transfers of ownership has increased correspondingly. Also, the Association produced a 16 mm motion picture film in color and sound giving considerable information on the origin, development and characteristics of the breed, as well as each of the five gaits at normal speed and slow motion. This film added a lot of interest at riding club meetings and animal husbandry classes at Universities.

Mike Cronan, grandson of "June" Cronan, writing in the September 2001 issue of *Equestrian* magazine said, "I can affirm his belief that the Saddlebred horse was ideally suited not just to the show ring, but also to trail riding, carriage pulling, cattle roping, fox hunting and just about anything else you might want to do with a horse." He had the **vision** to see the future of this Association.

Cronan was instrumental in the formation of the American Youth Council in **1968**. He served as Director of the American Horse Shows Association (AHSA), the United States Pony Club, the American Bred Pleasure Horse Association, American Horse Council, and Kentucky State Fox Hunters Association. He was a director of and a founder of the Oxmoor Steeplechase. In **1983** he received the Distinguished Service Award from the National Pedigreed Livestock Council. The Rock Creek Riding Club and Horse Show inducted him into the inaugural Hall of Fame.

Upon his retirement in **1983**, the Association gave him a plaque officially designating him "Mr. Saddlebred." This award had been preceded seven years earlier with his selection as "Horseman of the Year" by the United Professional Horsemen's Association.

In **1986** ASHA initiated the C. J. Cronan Sportsmanship Award. The recipients are chosen for their sportsmanship and their contributions to the breed. Such attributes considered are participation in ASHA, support of ASHA, and contributions to ASHA. Only male ASHA members are eligible.

Charles J. Cronan, Jr.

Allie G. Jones was honored with the Presidency of the American Saddle Horse Breeders' Association in **1936**. He was one of the most successful and constructive breeders of saddle horses. He bred and showed many of the most famous progeny in history and was considered to be greatest breeder and showman in his time. His farm was at North Middletown, Kentucky where he bred the immortal Bourbon King and many of his famous progeny.

Col. Thomas M. Wilson was elected in **1948** the President of the American Saddle Horse Breeders' Association on the death of A. G. Jones. He was one of the most prominent dealers and was a renowned judge. He had officiated at most of the important shows in the United States and Canada. He was a great horseman who had favored the saddle horse with his support for many years.

Susanne (pen name for Emily Ellen Scharf) – In **1948** came the loss of one of the most prolific American saddle horse writers. Susanne could describe a saddle horse contest with flair of words, explicit detail and excitement that made you feel that you were on the edge of your seat watching. It has been stated that Susanne was the uncrowned queen of historians for the Saddlebred horse breed. Her three volumes of *Famous Saddle Horses* are considered the **only authentic history of its development**.

Volume I was published in 1932 (509 pages) with selected stories about the most important saddle horses in the early days of the American saddle horse that she had written for the *Farmers Home Journal*. This first book was so successful that she had the third reprint to supply the demand. Volume II was published in 1942 (499 pages) when she was associated with the *American Horseman,* which she compiled and edited during her spare time which necessitated working as many as twenty hours a day. Volume III was published in 1947 (747 pages) after she resigned from *American Horseman* to bring the history of the breed up to date. Today, these are vintage books that are a reference for the breeder and exhibitor.

After the *Farmers Home Journal* folded during the depression, Susanne as Editor and J. H. Ransom as publisher launched the *Kentucky Horseman*. It was successful from the first issue and Ransom sold his interest to Matt Cohen who changed the name to the *American Horseman*.

J. H. Ransom published in **1948** *Who's Who and Where in Horsedom*, his first book in a seventeen volume set. He endeavored to make a reference book for all breeds of light horses with a classified directory of leading owners, breeders and the prominent stallions. It was his plan to publish histories of the prominent breeding farms and the famous horsemen in each volume that would contain all the interesting facts about these

famous farms and their owners. Every great American Saddlebred you've "ever" heard of is profiled in these magnificent books with outstanding vintage photographs. The last book was published in 1972 that ended a great resource of the golden years, as these books contain the stories behind the history of our breed. In 1958 Ransom said that his book had been lauded and supported by horsemen in 48 states and 19 foreign countries.

William Burke Belknap took over the Presidency of the American Saddle Horse Breeders' Association in **1958**. He bred Saddlebreds at his Land O' Goshen Farm, Goshen, KY. He was a driving force in establishing the Oldham County Fair in 1933. William had been a member of the Kentucky House of Representatives, 59th District, 1924-1928, 1934-1935. He was a descendant of the prominent Belknap family of merchants in Louisville.

Incorporators:

Mrs. Frank Goggin

Charles J. Cronan, Jr.

J. H. Ransom

H. B. Murray

Earl Teater

American Saddle Horse Museum
Spindletop Carriage House

2014 Officers
President
Tom Erffmeyer
1st Vice President
Amy Dix Rock
2nd Vice President
Bridget McNeese
Secretary
Elisabeth M. Goth
Treasurer
Joellen Blount

The **American Saddle Horse Museum**, a separate entity opened **July 12, 1962** in the carriage house at Spindletop Farm, Lexington, KY, formerly the property of Mrs. Pansy Yount of Beaumont, Texas. The Curator and guiding spirit of the Museum was Mrs. Frank Goggin a.k.a. Estheray Goggin of Lexington, KY. It later moved to Louisville, Kentucky, in 1977.

 **Thomas J. Morton, Jr**. was President of the American Saddle Horse Breeders' Association in **1966-1980**. Morton is widely regarded as the father of the modern plastics industry and is largely responsible for establishing Evansville's renowned "Plastic Valley" as the national center for plastics manufacturing. Much of his Old Stone House Saddlebred stock was destroyed in a fire which razed the stables at Newburgh, Indiana on Jan. 4, 1951.

Bill Thompson. publisher of *Saddle & Bridle* published in his magazine on **April 28, 1978**, an editorial on "The Last Stockholders Meeting." **Here, of late, this status quo has been somewhat disturbed with pressure from new breeders of Saddlebreds, who are becoming concerned with dismally low prices many of their colts are bringing at production sales. Better publicity for the breed has often been a complaint of breeders going back to 1909. For decades, the Breeders Association has registered fewer than 4000 new Saddlebreds, per year, while other breeds have started from nowhere and now register over 50,000 horses per year.**

ASHBA President **Thomas Morton** announced proudly that the stockholder membership had increased from 38 new members in 1976 to over 400 new members in 1977. The most pressing of issues was held to the last, and that was the matter of bringing the membership up to the current times. This was presented by Mr. Joseph E. Stopher who explained a new plan for annual membership instead of a stockholder membership. Under consideration for the past year with legal counsel, at long last this new membership system allows the association to dispense with the voting power of several thousand deceased stockholders by proxy, a chronic problem of the past.

In order to dispose of these deceased stockholder's stock, this unaccounted for stock was put up for sale at Public auction. This stock was purchased by the Association, and since it is no longer outstanding, a quorum of the remaining stockholders was obtained. The ASHBA was then able to amend its Articles of Incorporation and thereby adopt an **annual membership policy**, instead of a stockholder's membership. And so it was, after 87 years of existence with the original bylaws, the ASHBA has at long last made a change, perhaps one of the most important changes to be made since its incorporation.

With the amendment to the articles of incorporation made, the Association proceeded with its last Stockholder's meeting and elected six directors: Helen Crabtree, Cynthia Wood, Chat Nichols, Hugh Richardson, Mrs. William Roth, and Joseph E. Stopher

Tom Moore was the founding father of the United Professional Horsemen's Association (UPHA) in **1968** and was elected first President. The objective was **to establish an organization that would give a united voice to the horse professional** in order to better address concerns and problems that existed within the show horse industry and to improve conditions for all those involved.

UPHA has worked to improve horse shows by advising on such concerns as class scheduling, lighting and show ring footing. Grooms and caretakers, the backbone of the industry, have also benefited from a great improvement of the facilities provided for them at horse shows.

The life-size statue of Tom Moore was dedicated on Wednesday, August 10, 2005 in the gardens in front of Freedom Hall in Louisville. He was honored as the trainer who had won more championships at the World's Championship Horse Show than any other participant in the show's history. Tom was often called "The Tall Man" and in 1990 was selected as a member of the Kentucky State Fair Hall of Fame. He was a Director of ASHA, named Horseman of the Year in 1986 and 1994 by the American Horse Shows Association, now USA Equestrian, the only person to earn that honor twice.

Mexico, MO American Saddlebred Museum located in the Audrain County Historical Society Complex. Its official inception was in 1966 and the new building was opened in **1970. Janet Nesheim**, the first and only chair of the Society's horse museum committee, was directed by its Board of Directors "to make it happen" and she became the **Curator**. The museum has an extensive collection of artifacts and information. Mexico was once considered the "Saddlebred Horse Capital of the World" by Missourians. The museum features presentations on Tom Bass (a famous black horseman), George Ford Morris, Art Simmons (a local trainer) and Callaway Hills stallion, Will Shriver. The famous Saddlebred Horse, Rex McDonald, is buried on the grounds.

In **1980,** Tom Morton had served fourteen years as President of the American Saddle Horse Breeders' Association and wanted to step down. Tom and "June" Cronan agreed that **Jim Aikman** had been an aspiring Board member since 1966 and should be the new leader. They did not find Aikman receptive because of his responsibility to the family business of designing and providing Commercial Service facilities all over the world as the Aikman Company,

Indianapolis, IN. In addition, he owned Hide-A-Way Farms, Acton, IN that had a stallion in service and some mares that required his attention.

After continuous persuasion by Morton and Cronan, they were able to coerce Aikman to accept the Presidency for two or three years. This automatically made Jim a Trustee of American Horse Council and Director of American Horse Show Association.

In his first Board meeting, he asked the members, "What do you want to accomplish?" There were no answers. Jim is a man that has to know where he is going, what he can do and likes to set goals.

After a public announcement was made that Jim was President **1980-1983**, the phone started ringing with suggestions from all levels of the industry.

The Association's primary work had been to register and transfer horses. The obvious need was to promote the horse but the office had not been staffed for promotion. We need to make people want to buy a Saddlebred horse. Jim Blackwell, who had been the Executive Secretary of the American Horse Show Association, had already been hired. Jim Aikman recognized that "June" Cronan (who had been made Executive Vice President in 1979) and Jim Blackwell needed additional help.

To expand the Association, an appeal was sent out for an Executive Secretary. Aikman got a phone call from his old friend Dick Morgan, Denver, CO. Dick wanted the position. He was well educated, very articulate, known for his expertise in announcing horse shows and had great exposure to the workings of other breed organizations. This was invaluable as the Association did not have to reinvent the wheel when Dick came on board.

With the recommendation of Jim Aikman, the ASHA Board approved Dick Morgan as Executive Secretary. Dick Morgan was a tremendous contributor to bringing new ideas to the ASHA. Progress commenced when Dick Morgan explained the potential of Youth Groups and Charter Clubs. Dick Morgan brought the Youth Club to the floor while Jim Aikman was President. The Youth Club was formed and Aikman asked Bonnie Mercuri of Centerville, Ohio to Chair the first Youth program. She served as National Chairperson of the American Saddlebred Youth Organization and was a member of the Ohio State 4-H Horse Committee for many years.

The registry had been growing in number of horses and members, the name American Saddle Horse Breeders' Association no longer reflected the expanding functions of the Association. Therefore, on **April 22, 1980**, the registry's name was changed to American Saddlebred Horse Association (ASHA).

ASHA accepted responsibility of the **Broodmare Hall of Fame** in **1981** that had been established in 1972 as a project of the Southeastern Futurity. A committee, consisting of Jim Aikman, Mae Condon, Carl Fischer, Don Stafford, Lynn Weatherman, Linda Graham Leonard, and Judy Werner was formed. Criteria for inclusion in this group of elite mares were established; some of the qualities desired included: having produced champion show horses and/or sons or daughters important in the breeding world; being prolific; and having representatives in the breed today.

Jim Aikman wanted to improve communication through a newsletter. Dick Morgan with his wife Mary Lou went to work on a newsletter and the final result was the *American Saddlebred* magazine that was started in **1982**. This was the vehicle to promote the Saddlebred. Jim felt if they were going any place they needed computers. They purchased a computer program from Walter Bush whose foresight started computers in breeding.

Jim Aikman had the insight to perceive that the Board membership should be changed. Some of the members lived too far away from Louisville to attend the meetings, were committed to other businesses and it was time for younger members to serve on the Board. He took on the task of asking several older members to retire. These gentlemen were agreeable and this allowed Jim to bring to the board Dr. Simon Fredericks and Carl Fischer. This was a major move in restructuring the Board.

One of Jim Aikman's personal concerns was the set tail of yearlings in Futurities. For participants to be competitive, they had to cut the tail, but this was a disadvantage for the amateur. A tail must be taken care when it is cut and an amateur who works cannot do this and too often the tail would slip to one side and the yearling was ruined for life. Aikman presented a rule that the tails not be cut to the ASHA board and it was accepted. The next year there were 30 yearlings entered in the Futurity at the Kentucky State Fair compared to 8 the previous year.

With the increase in staff there was not enough space, not enough restrooms and the old building was in disrepair. The staff started looking for available office space in Louisville. After looking at several possible sites in Louisville, Jim was able to convince the board that they should move to the Kentucky Horse Park. This was the biggest accomplishment during Jim's Presidency.

Shortly after, in **1983**, Jim received a phone call from Alvin Ruxer, stating that his great stallion, Supreme Sultan, was very ill with colic. After their conversation, Jim being a realist thought the stallion would not recover so he called Wallace Wilkerson (head of the Kentucky Horse Park) and asked him for permission to bury Supreme Sultan there. His wish was granted and when the grieving Ruxer called back to notify the death of the stallion, Jim was able to tell him of the arrangements he had made and Alvin was very pleased.

Jim Aikman exemplified the characteristics of a **visionary** for the American Saddlebred Horse Association. He is a man with a "servant's heart" and knows how to make things happen. He was always one step ahead of his contemporaries. His leadership contributed to the advancement of the Association during his three years as President. In 1989 Jim Aikman received the C. J. Cronan Sportsmanship Award. In 1995 he was inducted into the World's Championship Hall of Fame and in 2006 he received the Lifetime Achievement Award from the American Saddlebred Horse Association.

Irene Zane, manager of Sunnyslope Farm, Scott City, Kansas, in 1957 was a founder of the American Saddlebred Pleasure Horse Association and was the President for eight years. She had been credited with beginning the Saddlebred pleasure horse movement. The ASPHA was instrumental in promoting ASBs as pleasure horses primarily through the tireless efforts of **Irene Zane**. In **1983**, the American Saddlebred Horse Association took over the duties of the **American Saddlebred Pleasure Horse Association** regarding the promotion of American Saddlebred horses as pleasure mounts.

American Saddle Horse Breeders' Assoc.
929 South Fourth St., Louisville, KY

American Saddle Horse Museum
730 West Main St., Louisville, KY

Collectively, the American Saddle Horse Breeders' Association and the American Saddle Horse Museum recognized that they needed to move. The lack of sufficient space by the Association, the lack of visitor interest in the Museum location and operating from deteriorating buildings made the relocation to the Kentucky Horse Park, Lexington, KY a top priority. The move in location brought the establishment of innovative promotional and educational programs for the further development of the American Saddlebred horse. The Kentucky Horse Park is the world's only park dedicated to man's relationship with the horse.

When Dick Morgan returned to being a horse show announcer, **Kathy Eggan** was brought in to be Executive Secretary. She was involved in getting the records computerized and planning the space and equipment for the move to the Kentucky Horse Park.

Dr. Simon Fredricks of Houston, TX; his appointment to the Board of ASHA was timely because he was a **man of vision** and business acumen. He was an internationally well-known and respected Plastic Surgeon, founder of the prestigious American Society of Aesthetic Plastic Surgeons, President of that organization, President of the Plastic Surgery Educational Foundation as well as the Aesthetic Surgery Educational and Research Foundation. Dr. Fredricks was engaged in active practice in Houston, served as Full Clinical Professor of Plastic Surgery at Baylor College of Medicine as well as the University of Texas Medical Branch Houston.

Simon started the Simbara Farms Saddlebred breeding program in 1981 and in 38 years the Simbara brand was known throughout the industry when there was a dispersal sale at Tattersall's. His successful breeding operation was honored with the Breeders Hall of Fame Award in 2004 by ASHA. Simon was President of the American Saddle Horse Museum Feb. 1988- Feb. 1992.

When Simon attended his first ASHA Board meeting he voiced his opinion that the new location of the ASHA offices should be in the Kentucky Horse Park and asked to be given time to check with the Horse Park. His motion was granted and he called the Chairman of Board at Kentucky Horse Park, Wallace Wilkerson. The possibility of having ASHA offices at the Horse Park intrigued Mr. Wilkerson as it gave him mobility to get some action. This was a time when critics thought the Horse Park was a white elephant. Dr. Fredricks explained that he wanted a site that was visible when visitors drove into the Horse Park. He chose a site knowing that an arena was going to be built behind it and this added to the visibility.

Dr. Fredricks was the Chairman of the Building Committee and was given a free hand. He contacted a major builder in Louisville, KY who had two building companies, one was non-union. Dr. Fredricks chose the non-union building company that was more cost effective. He hired an architect firm and a design firm. The design had to be compatible with the other buildings in the park. Simon wanted a theatre in the museum that would hold a bus load of kids and he insisted that there be a gift shop, but the park required a limited space because there was already a gift shop at the park.

William M. Schaefer   Alvin C. Ruxer

One of the responsibilities of Dr. Fredricks was to raise money to pay for the new building. The initial contribution was from William M. Schaefer, Londonville, N.Y. who gave $500,000.

24

Schaefer amassed multiple World's Championship titles during the 1980's and 90's, but is best remembered for the pair of grand fine harness horses, CH Shadow's Creation and CH Supreme Odyssey, shown by Bill and Gwen respectively.

Obtaining a mortgage on a commercial property with a lease, without any assets, was not a standard procedure. However, **Alvin C. Ruxer** of Jasper, IN came forward to carry the mortgage. Some years later when the mortgage had been paid down, a miracle happened. Ruxer decided to forgive one-half of the mortgage and donate the other one-half to UPHA. This good deed shows the generosity of Alvin C. Ruxer.

Alvin C. Ruxer was the founder of Jasper Engine & Transmission Exchange, Ruxer Ford and Jasper State Bank and built an American Saddlebred horse farm that was known throughout the nation. His great stallion, Supreme Sultan, became a legend, a hero and a sire that changed the look of the Saddlebred forever. As of 2004, he was the only sire to have World Grand Champions in all the show divisions.

Most building programs run into a problem along the way. Simon Fredricks had to contend with a power-to-be of the Horse Park that called him and said that the site location would have to be changed because it interfered with visibility of the arena that was going to be built. Simon told him that he had already raised the building money and his donors would sue him if there was a change and in turn he would have to sue the Horse Park. This statement satisfied the retention of the site chosen.

Joseph E. Stopher, Attorney, and Dr. Fredricks were the negotiating team. They signed a contract with Governor John Y. Brown for a 99 year lease at $1 per year.

The new building was built by the American Saddle Horse Museum because it was a 501 (c) (3) non-profit corporation and donations could be tax deductible whereby that did not apply to the Association at that time.

Judy Werner of Waterloo, IL, accepted the Presidency of ASHA and served from **1984-1992**. She was the first woman to hold this position. Judy and her husband Roy own Redwing Farm, a full service breeding farm offering year round care for broodmares and their offspring with Designed currently heading the farm's breeding program.

Judy was a strong supporter of saddle seat riding with the American Saddlebred as the ultimate show horse and a strong advocate of the American Saddlebred being used for other disciplines. She has been an active member of UPHA and the American Horse Council.

The **ASR Grand National**, begun in **1984**, was popular with youth and amateur exhibitors and Saddlebred pleasure horse proponents. It was open to any aged horse sired by an ASR Grand National Nominated Sire.

Saddlebred Grand National costs $500-$1,500 to nominate a horse to (depending on the age of the horse) and they must be sired by a nominated sire (whose owner paid to have him nominated). Grand National pays out to the horse's current owner, the person who paid the initial recording fee for the horse, and the person who paid the nominating fee for the stallion if these people were current ASHA members. The Grand National Committee of ASR recommended the termination of the Grand National Program and it was dissolved in **2012**. This decision by the ASR Board and Grand National Committee is the result of a decline in Grand National horse recordings and stallion nominations over the last ten years.

Keith D. Bartz, with his wife Carol, owned and operated Hollow Haven Farm at Chanhassen, MN for 27 years, where they helped many amateurs and juvenile riders reach success in the show ring. **1984** was a pivotal year when Keith was asked to be a fund raiser for the new American Saddle Horse Museum in Lexington, KY.

It was because of his dedication to the American Saddlebred horse that he left his farm to get involved in a new challenge. Within nine months he became Executive Director and managed the Museum during an important period ending in **1998**. After his retirement, he served on the Board of Trustees from 2003 to 2009.

Keith started the fund raising from a part-time office in the Association's Louisville office. He found fund raising a daunting task. Committees were formed for soliciting but were not as effective as anticipated. The process was slow but a number of large contributors donated. Two successful plans were: **Honor your Horse With a Brick in the Museum's Saddlebred Sidewalk for $100 brick and Recognize Someone Who Loves the American Saddlebred with a Tile in the Walk of Honor for $250 tile.**

During the construction and development period, Keith would deal with payment of partial process bills, work with designer firms that did not know the Saddlebred horse industry, supervise construction of exhibits and attend giant meetings, etc.

When the mortgage got down to $400,000, there was a unique plan to pay off the balance. A Mortgage Redemption Committee was formed with 40 members. Each was asked to give $10,000 and this resolved the indebtedness.

After twelve strenuous years of administration at the Museum, Keith Bartz wanted to retire but this was not agreeable with the Trustees. He agreed to stay on for two more years if he could tele-commute from Nov. 1 to May 1 from Naples, FL. This plan was accepted and he retired on Nov. 1, 1998.

In 1973, Bartz was chosen "Horseperson of the Year" by Minnesota Horse Council. He served as Vice President of United Professional Horsemen's Association in 1975 and 1976 and President in 1977 and 1978. In 1981 he was Zone 6 Committee Chairman for the American Horse Show Association. Bartz also served as an active American Saddlebred Horse Association judge for 11 divisions until his retirement in 1998.

Keith received the C. J. Cronan Sportsmanship Award in 2005 and the Wing Commander Medal in 2011 from ASHA. Bartz served many years on the Board of Directors of the United States Equestrian Federation. For his outstanding sportsmanship, Bartz was the recipient of the USEF's Walter B. Devereux Sportsmanship Award in 2003. For his undying support and incredible legacy, Bartz was honored on his 80th birthday with the 2013 USEF Lifetime Achievement Award and he received the Jimmy A. Williams Lifetime Achievement Trophy (his trademark was his hat) at the Pegasus Awards gala. The trophy is a silver cowboy hat as worn in this photo and is symbolic of the Lifetime Achievement Award.

The revitalization of the ASHA continued under the direction of Judy Werner. Shortly after becoming President, Kathy Eggan the Executive Secretary resigned and she put together a search committee that hired **Pat Nichols** in **1985** who with her husband Chat had operated a successful training barn in Illinois.

Pat Nichols proved to be an able programs like Charter Clubs, of Fame (BHF), Champion (CH), blood typing, approval of the use centennial celebration and she of stallion service reports. administrator by supporting Youth Clubs, Brood Mare Hall overseas marketing, established of transported semen, the suggested the implementation

Pat hired Lynn Weatherman, Mae Condon, Lisa Duncan, Carrie Mortensen, Charlotte Tevis and Dede Gatlin, they worked as a competent team. Pat retired in **1996 a**nd received the ASHA Meritorious Service Award in **1997**.

Mae Condon, assistant to Pat Nichols, was given the assignment to interact with the **Charter Clubs**. Because of her background as former board member on the American Saddle Horse Breeder's Futurity of Wisconsin, she had an awareness of the contributions and the challenges of the Charter Clubs. During this time the Charter Club network was growing and the number of Charter Club members was increasing. Charter clubs play a vital role in the expansion of the breed by recognizing all Saddlebred owners and encouraging them to join the area clubs.

The ASHA **Charter Clubs** have developed into a worldwide network of more than 50 Charter Clubs enriching the American Saddlebred experience for members. Clubs promote American Saddlebreds at the local level and help newcomers to learn more about the breed, as well as offering many equine and social activities for their members' education and enjoyment. Typical activities for Charter Clubs include putting on horse shows, riding in parades, participating in horse fairs, presenting annual awards, trail rides and other popular pastimes.

ASHA **Youth Club** is the perfect place to meet other young people interested in horses, and the perfect way to become involved with American Saddlebreds. ASHA Youth Club members do not need to own a horse or even be taking riding lessons to participate. Any young person who likes horses is welcome!

In addition to a wide variety of activities and projects, both entertaining and educational, membership in an ASHA Youth Club provides the opportunity to participate in all the ASHA youth programs as well as trail rides, farm visits, clinics, horse shows and other horse-related adventures.

ASHA has strong and vibrant youth programs offering something for everyone. **Youth Programs** include Saddle Time, Academy Awards, ASHA Driving Challenge, Junior Judging, ASHA Youth Scholarships, and the American Saddlebred International Youth Program.

ASHA's **Saddlebred Record program** established the identification **CH** for successful breeding combinations. The prefix means **Champion** and becomes an actual part of the horse's registered name after 15 points have been earned in recognized competition. This name indicates the Saddlebred horse has been certified an official Champion by the American Saddlebred Horse Association.

Blood Typing was established that required a foal to be blood typed at the age of six weeks or later for permanent registration. The sire and dam must be registered American Saddlebreds with blood types on file. One must be a member of the association to do business with ASHA.

Overseas Marketing began when Sam Brannon organized the American Saddlebred's first trip overseas to Equitana in Essen, Germany, the largest horse fair in the world. ASHA had a Saddlebred booth there for several years.

Saddlebred Stallion Service Report is due in to the American Saddlebred Registry (ASR) no later than October 31 of the year during which the stallion is bred. In accordance with ASR Rule III. F., the owner or manager of a registered American Saddlebred stallion which has been bred to any registered American Saddlebred mare(s) during a breeding season must submit.

In **1985, ASHA headquarters moved** from Louisville, Kentucky, into the lower offices of the new American Saddle Horse Museum building. ASHA was the first horse breed registry to call the Kentucky Horse Park home. The American Saddlebred Horse Museum officially opened on **July 6th, 1986**, as the first horse bred museum in the park.

The life size bronze statue of **Supreme Sultan** on his grave
beautifully sculptured by Patricia Crane.

September 25, 1985 was a momentous occasion for the unveiling of the statue of Supreme
Sultan. Gov. Martha Lane Collins and Saddlebred dignitaries were present with about three
hundred or four hundred people there.

In the interim period, "June" Cronan, had died in 1984. A musician played the guitar and sang
"Danny Boy." "Mr. Saddlebred" was an Irishman and there was not a dry eye remembering his
contributions to the Association, the Breed and setting the Vision for the future.

Jim Aikman was the featured speaker and he gave a tribute to Charles J. Cronan, Jr. and the
magnificent breeding stallion Supreme Sultan. Alvin C. Ruxier, owner of Ruxier Farms, Jasper,
IN, established this stallion to be a great sire and the statistics were overwhelming. His
offspring became World Champions in all divisions. Supreme Sultan's breeding success has not
been equaled in this modern era.

When Jim Aikman got to a designated place in the address, Bill Caldwell who had been the
breeding manager for the stallion, slowly pulled the tarpaulin back; it was a "touching moment"
to see the life size bronze statue that Patricia Crane had created. Now the Supreme Sultan
monument fronts the American Saddlebred Museum for thousands of visitors from all over the
world to admire.

KENTUCKY HORSE PARK

The Saddlebred pleasure horse movement was enhanced in **1987** when actor **William Shatner** developed a western pleasure class for plain shod Saddlebreds. The Saddlebred is shown at a flat walk, jog trot and lope on a reasonably loose rein without undue restraint ridden with one hand on reins. Judged 75% on manners, performance, presence and quality and 25% on total conformation and neatness of attire. The Shatner Western Pleasure Championship is held every

September at the St. Louis National Charity Horse Show. In 1997 Saddle & Bridle magazine received a trademark for SADDLE & BRIDLE'S ASB SHATNER WESTERN PLEASURE CLASS as a sponsor.

Beginning in **1991**, ASHA **Scholarships** are awarded yearly to students involved with the Saddlebred industry as a means to fulfill one of ASHA's principle missions – the education and encouragement of youths. These scholarships are available to applicants who are ASHA members, have completed grade 11, are under age 21 and who best meet the qualifications of financial need, academic success, commitment to the American Saddlebred and ASHA youth programs

1991 Centennial Celebration RESOLUTION IN THE SENATE OF THE UNITED STATES
July 18 (legislative day, JULY 8), 1991.

Whereas today there are more than 75,000 living pedigree American Saddlebred horses on record at the American Saddlebred Horse Association;

Whereas the breed is heralded internationally as the ultimate show horse, demonstrating animation, brilliance, and grace at 3 and 5 gaits, as well as excelling as a pleasure and driving horse;

Whereas there are more than 7,000 active members of the American Saddlebred Horse Association and 56 affiliated American Saddlebred Horse Association Charter Clubs that exhibit the breed at an estimated 1,000 annual horse shows, fairs, and special events throughout the United States, Canada, Australia, and Europe; and

Whereas the American Saddlebred Horse Association will be holding a `Centennial Celebration' for thousands of members and spectators during the week of the Kentucky State Fair World Championship Horse Show, the Saddlebred sport's premier event: Now, therefore, be it Resolved, That in recognition of the centennial year of the American Saddlebred Horse Association and of the role played by this distinguished breed in the history and growth of our great Nation, the week of August 18, 1991, through August 24, 1991, is designated as `**National American Saddlebred Horse Week'.**

ASHA Little Saddlers from the Rock Creek Riding Club and Jim B. Robertson Stables performing during the Centennial Celebration at the Kentucky State Fair World Championship Horse Show,

Transported semen was approved by ASR on March 1, 1991. Breeding is allowed by the use of transported semen which is defined as any breeding by artificial insemination which takes place at a location other than the premises where the stallion from which semen is used is standing. Fresh cooled or frozen semen may be used. The use of frozen semen collected from a stallion that had died or been castrated after January 1, 1995 will be allowed. The Registry must receive notification signed by a licensed veterinarian within 30 days of the death or castration of the stallion.

Randi Stuart Wightman of Tulsa, OK served as President of ASHA from **1993 to 1996.** In 1963 Randi won the American Horse Shows Association Medal Final and in 1964 received the National Horse Show "Good Hands" Final. At the age of only nineteen, Randi received the 1967 "Horsewoman of the Year" Award from the American Horse Shows Association (USEF) – the first amateur Saddlebred rider so honored.

At the World's Championship Horse Show in 2005, Randi was inducted into the Hall of Fame. Her wisdom, experience and knowledge of the industry was a benefit to the Association.

<h2 style="text-align:center">Saddlebred "Triple Crown"</h2>

Harold Morgeson, who served an of Rock Creek Riding Club, years ago, "The Rock Creek Horse Horse Show in July, and the Championship Horse Show in Saddlebred horse what the **"Triple**

unprecedented 17 terms as President Louisville, KY, made a statement Show, the Lexington Junior League Kentucky State Fair World August, are to the American **Crown"** is to the thoroughbred.

Harold was known as "Mr. Rock Creek" and was an ardent Kentuckian. Later this idea was fulfilled with the UPHA American Royal National Championship Horse Show, Kansas City, MO. It was held in November and actually became the third leg of the "Triple Crown" in place of Morgeson's Rock Creek.

Lexington Junior League Horse Show, Lexington, KY

The Lexington Junior League was founded in 1924 to promote voluntarism among women and support the Lexington community. These ladies realized that most of their fundraisers only made about $900, which didn't go very far at the time, when people where in such desperate need of help. In **1937** they established the Charity Horse Show that attracted 216 horses from 16 states, and 24,000 spectators. When the bills were paid and the books balanced, the profit was $5,500.

The horse show has grown to be the world's largest outdoor American Saddlebred show and the **first leg of the Saddlebred "Triple Crown".** It is held at The Red Mile harness racing track. Today, the show attracts approximately 1,000 world recognized competitors from the U.S. and Canada, has raised over four million dollars for charitable and civic organizations in Central Kentucky and generates over 5 million dollars in revenue for local merchants each summer. The Lexington Jr. League Charity Horse Show has truly made a tremendous impact in Saddlebred industry; as well as, in the local community.

It is a tribute to the ladies of the Junior League of Lexington for the success of this prestigious event with regular attendance of around 30,000 people each year and attracts nationally renowned competitors.

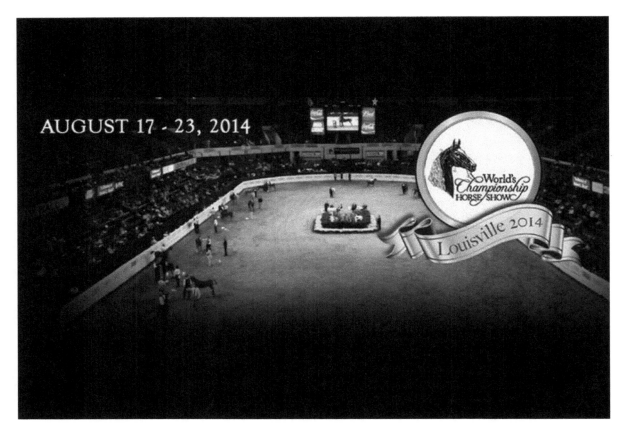

AUGUST 17 - 23, 2014

World's Championship HORSE SHOW
Louisville 2014

Kentucky State Fair World Championship Horse Show, Louisville, KY

The World's Championship Horse Show, the second leg of the Saddlebred "Triple Crown," the **world's richest and most prestigious horse show**, attracts spectators and competitors from across the world. It includes over 2,000 horses competing for more than $1 million in awards. It began in 1902 at Churchill Downs. Before Louisville was picked to become the permanent site of the Kentucky State Fair in 1906, the fair was held in Owensboro and Lexington.

Construction for an amphitheater at the then-named State Fairgrounds began in 1906 and until it was finished in 1908, the fair and horse show was held at Churchill Downs. In 1908, the $100,000 amphitheater was finished and for the first time, in 1909, the show was held at night under lights and automobiles filled the parking lots.

The first $10,000 Five-Gaited World's Grand Championship, which would forever be the high point of the show, began in 1917. The 1950s saw construction of the new Kentucky State Fairgrounds and in 1956 the first performance of the World's Championship Horse Show was held in Freedom Hall. For the first time in 1971, more than 1,000 horses were entered in the Kentucky State Fair Horse Show. Premiums for the World's Championship Horse Show reached more than $200,000 in 1978. In 1993 for the first time in history, the awards and premiums for the World's Championship Horse Show exceeded $1 million.

Photo by Chris Willis

UPHA American Royal National Championship Horse Show, Kansas City, MO

The UPHA American Royal National Championship Horse Show is proud to be the **oldest continuous Saddlebred show** in the world. The show began in 1894 through the collaboration of an unlikely pair: Tom Bass, the legendary African-American horse trainer, and Arthur Stilwell, a civic leader in Independence, Missouri. The first show was held in Independence before moving to the Convention Hall in Kansas City. At the turn of the century, the Saddle Horse show became part of the newly created American Royal Livestock and Horse Show. The Kemper Arena is the home for the National horse show.

Considered the third leg of the American Saddlebred "Triple Crown," this show is the grand finale of both the American Royal season and the last national Saddlebred show of the year. A historic partnership between the UPHA and the American Royal in 2002 has produced remarkable growth and excitement for this show, bringing new participants, fans and the best horses and riders to Kansas City.

After the retirement of Pat Nichols as Executive Secretary, **Dottie Dobbs** and **Marcia Carothers** followed in that ASHA position.

The **ASHA Year-End Awards**, a program initiated in **1997**, lists all the winners in various sport horse disciplines of open, purebred and part-bred dressage, driving, hunter, jumper, eventing, distance riding and sport horse in-hand competitions.

Tom C. Pettry took over the reins of the Presidency of ASHA from **1997-2001**. Tom had a corporate advertising background. He and his wife Jeanne and their children Donna, Kristen, Tom D. and Andrew have all been exhibitors in virtually every Saddlebred division over the years. In 2005 the Thomas Pettry Family were inducted into St. Louis National Charity Horse Show Hall Of Fame. In 2007 the Pettry/Fergusson Family received the Paul and Dorothy Gillenwater Family Award from ASHA.

Tolley Graves became Executive Director of the **American Saddle Horse Museum** in **1999**. She succeeded Keith D. Bartz who had owned Hollow Haven Farm where she received riding instructions as a teenager. Tolley had been an owner, breeder and exhibitor of American Saddlebreds since childhood. She was a graduate of Northwestern University. She had administrative experience as an Assistant at the Kentucky Tourist Commission and was Executive Director of the Harrodsburg Main Street Program that worked for the historic preservation and revitalization of downtown Harrodsburg, KY.

Tolley's executive skills were revealed in her writing of the script for the 25-minute film, "The Spindletop Legacy" that won the Bronze International Telly Award in 2004. Again, in 2007 Tolley and Curator, Kim Skipton, produced a 30-minute film, "Out of the Shadows" that was awarded a Silver International Telly Award, the highest prize offered. This film featured "Bringing to Light Black Horseman in Saddlebred History."

The Museum's Mission Statement calls for the organization to **"present the traditions and heritage of the American Saddlebred Horse through the collection, preservation, and display of artifacts, fine art, photography and the written word."** Tolley likes to refer to the Museum "as the Showplace for Saddlebreds" because "it attempts to show the breed off to its best advantage through exciting permanent and changing exhibits." This $3.5 million facility became the **American Saddlebred Museum in 2000.**

ASHA members who have served as President of the Museum have been:

1961-1962 R.C. Tway	Feb. 1984-Feb. 1988 Roz Harris
1962-1967 Dr. H.B. Murray	Feb. 1988-Feb. 1992 Dr. Simon Fredricks
1967-1970 Dr. Donald Jacobs	Feb. 1992-Feb. 1995 Lanny Greer
1970-1973 Earl (Pete) Teater, Jr.	Feb. 1995-Feb. 2000 John Lenore
1973-1975 Redd Crabtree	Feb. 2000-Feb. 2004 Mary Ann Pardieck

1975-1977 Mel Peavey

1977-1982 Dr. Donald Jacobs

1982-1984 J. Wingate Brown

Feb. 2004-Feb. 2009 Albert E. Dix

Feb. 2009-Feb. 2013 Laurel Nelson

Feb. 2013-Tom Erffmeyer

Fred. K. Sarver of Carlisle, KY was President of ASHA for the full allowable term from **2002-2007**. He is owner of Cornerstone Farm, Carlisle, KY, a modern breeding facility. Fred has been President of ASR, Vice President of ASM, Second Vice President of UPHA, Vice Chairman of Virginia Equine Center Foundation and Vice President of Virginia Horse Center Foundation. He received the C. J. Cronan Sportsmanship Award and was inducted into Virginia Horse Center Hall of Fame in 2009.

A bright idea was conceived by **Jim Aikman** in **2002** with the **All American Cup** (AAC) that has put blood and life "back" into the American Saddlebred Breeding Industry. Jim is the American Saddlebred horseman of renown that believes in the "maternal influence" in breeding and documents this theory on CD. The All American Cup is a Limited Breeders Stake for Weanlings and 3 Year Old American Saddlebred Horses that is held each year in two (2) divisions Weanlings and 3 Year Old Open classes. The classes are held annually at the All American Horse Classic (AAHC), Indiana State Fairgrounds, Indianapolis, Indiana.

The funding for the All American Cup classes comes from the sale of Stallion Services that have been donated by stallion owners and are sold at the All American Cup Auction. A starting bid of $500 has been guaranteed by the Stallion Service Donor. The next bid must be $600, with each subsequent bid a minimum of $50. Stallions may be nominated to the All American Cup by the owner donating one Stallion Service to the annual auction. Stallion owners who donate a breeding fee to the All American Cup may also declare one mare in foal to the Stallion, at a cost equal to the exact amount that was paid for the Service in the auction, but not to exceed $800. The resulting foal will be eligible for both the Weanling and Three Year Old divisions of the American Cup.

In the beginning, the All American Cup Stallion Service Auction was held at Claudia Sanders Restaurant, Shelbyville, KY. Starting in 2008 a tour was given to review stallions at nearby Kentucky Saddlebred farms. The 2014 ACC Review and Stallion Service auction was held at Dr. Scott and Linda Bennett's Alliance Stud Farm, Simpsonville, KY. This was presented like an extravaganza show with food, music and entertainment provided. The large arena was split in half with one side for seating and the other set up for the preview of stallions. There were 18 stallions shown as the "voice," Peter Fenton, gave a little bit of back ground on each stallion and the crowd whooped and hollered while each stallion had his own theme song played.

The signature promoter, Jim Aikman, had an added incentive for the stallion service donor and buyer. After the last stallion service was sold, there was a drawing for an $18,000 All American Cup/Eclipse Aluminum Breeders' Deluxe Trailer. A record $204,750 was realized from the sale of 143 stallion services. **The All American Cup is the largest paying event in Saddlebred history** having paid out a world record $2,271,373 since inception. American Saddlebred enthusiasts will be impressed of how the wizard, Jim Aikman, has put together gifted personnel and generous supporters to develop the biggest program ever offered to the owners, breeders, trainers of the American Saddlebred from one little office at his Hide-Away-Farm. But, Jim says, "doesn't do nuthin'."

In 2012 with Jim Aikman's endorsement there was a major move in the horse world with the bonding of the All American Cup and Sport Horse Versatility Series. There was the premier of two new classes, a Hunter Pleasure Prospect Class, and a Western Pleasure Prospect class, at the All American Cup. These classes are open to any three or four year old American Saddlebreds fillies or geldings who were bred through stallions services purchased through the All American Cup Stallion Service Auction. This prize money, which is derived from a completely separate fund from the All American Cup Futurity, has been raised by Aikman.

DNA Testing is necessary to verify parentage. All breeding stallions must have DNA test results on file at ASR. All mares producing horses for which an Application for Registration is submitted on or after **January 1, 2003**, must have DNA test results on file. DNA testing requires either submission of a new blood sample or conversion of frozen serum on file at a **Registry** approved laboratory to DNA. All testing will be at the expense of the recorded owner.

Alan F. Balch took over the position in April **2004**. He had been President Trust and President of National a Charter Club Council was formed an important part of the nationwide of Executive Secretary/Registrar of USAE, Pres. of USA Equestrian Horse Show. During his tenure and Charter Clubs were to become marketing. The Council would recognize American Saddlebred horses in each region that excelled in a discipline. Awards were given at the end of the year. This opened the market for American Saddlebred's who may not have the potential to be a star on the green shavings. Alan resigned in February 2010.

Misdee Wrigley (Miller), Director of ASHA, was appointed by ASHA President Fred Sarver, to serve on the Board of KEEP (Kentucky Equine Education Project) that was formed in 2004. KEEP has the leadership of former Governor Brereton Jones, to foster education of the Kentucky public and legislature as to the importance of all equine breeds and activities to the economy and future of the state. It was essential that the American Saddlebred be represented.

Misdee is a fourth generation horsewoman who owns the multi-breed Hillcroft Farm in Paris, KY. She has American Saddlebred horses, Dutch Harness horses, Hackney horses, polo ponies, and a collection of antique carriages.

Fast forward, Misdee Wrigley married James Miller on September 15th, 2006 at beautiful Hillcroft Farm. In 2005, she was Treasurer of KOSBA. Misdee was First Vice President of the ASHA Board of Directors in 2006-2007 and recipient of the ASHA Lurline Roth Sportsmanship Award in 2009. She has served as President of the World Coaching Club, Trustee of the United States Equestrian Team Foundation, served on the Board of the Kentucky Horse Park Foundation, and the Kentucky Governor's Advisory Committee for the World Equestrian Games.

Assisted Reproduction, effective **Feb. 21, 2004** by ASR, there are no limitations on the number of foals that may be registered per donor mare. "Assisted Reproduction" refers to any process by which an embryo or oocyte is transferred from its genetic dam (the donor mare) to another mare (the carrier mare), which acts as the host and carries the foal. This process includes, but is not limited to, embryo transplant, oocyte transplant and in vitro fertilization.

In **2005**, by means of an **internal corporate reorganization** of the functions of the Registry and a companion organization previously named the American Saddlebred Horse Association Foundation, the American Saddlebred Horse Association, a public charity organized under section 501 (c)(3) of the Internal Revenue Code which allows donors to deduct contributions, became the breed's membership organization. All functions of the Registry now formally reside in the American Saddlebred Registry, a separate corporation organized under section 501 (c)(5) of the Internal Revenue Code which allows administration of prize programs. The 18 directors of the Association, of which 6 are elected each year to 3-year terms, elect the 9 directors of the Registry, each of whom serves an annual term.

In **2006**, ASHA **Charter Council** was formed to create more efficient communication channels between ASHA Charter Clubs and the ASHA Board of Directors. This Council will work to give a stronger voice to Charter Clubs within the ASHA structure, as well as give Charter Clubs more direct contact to the Board of Directors. President Fred Sarver named ASHA Director **Nancy Boone** of Concord, NC, the liaison from the Board of Directors to the newly formed Charter Club Council. Boone was selected because of her willingness to serve and as a result of her great dedication to her local charter club, the American Saddlebred Association of the Carolinas (ASAC). Boone has been a member of ASAC since 1981 and has served a number of roles within the 700-member charter club, including treasurer, director, youth advisor and vice president. In 2013 Nancy received the ASHA Meritorious Service Award.

In **2007** three principals of **Saddlebred Rescue, Inc**. (SBR), <u>Pat Johnson</u>, <u>Nealia McCracken</u> and <u>Christy Parker</u> were given the "Heroes for Horses" award by USEF. This award is presented to an individual(s) or organization(s) that have demonstrated an unwavering commitment to the protection and welfare of horses and/or have saved equines through an act of courage and resolve.

Interest in saving Saddlebreds from the slaughter house evolved from an Internet discussion group. Christy Parker, owner/trainer at Pine Haven Stables in Brunswick, GA, created a new 501(c)(3) charitable corporation, Saddlebred Rescue, Inc. along with a corresponding web site www.saddlebredrescue.com. At the same time, New Jersey trainer Nealia McCracken and Pat Johnson began to spend their Mondays at New Holland Sales Stable in New Holland, Pennsylvania looking for Saddlebreds in need.

In 2006 Nealia McCracken joined forces with Christy Parker and soon thereafter, the physical operations part of the rescue was moved to McCracken's 40 acre horse farm, North Wind Stables, Hardwick, NJ. Since its inception, Saddlebred Rescue has purchased over **800 horses from auctions** that were destined for slaughter, rehabbed them, and placed them in new forever homes.

Some of the horses at Saddlebred Rescue rehab that they recycle are used Amish horses that otherwise would have been sent to Canada and Mexico to the slaughter plants. They discovered as others have that the used horses from the Amish have a lot yet to give, while before their fate had few options. Previously these communities had few options other than to sell their horses to slaughter. What this rescue group has discovered is that many of these horses make wonderful lesson horses, trail horses and pleasure horses.

American Horse Adoption operated by Saddlebred Rescue, Inc. is a truly unique rescue that incorporates the thinking and practices of a professional show stable with the realities of the plight of unwanted horses today. SBR buys all horses in the program mostly from auctions and sales where they were slaughter bound. They have a professional trainer who works with each horse to evaluate and design a schooling program to help the horse be as adoptable as possible. All horses in the program are evaluated by two professional horse trainers before they are placed. Then American Horse Adoption works hard to find new forever homes and match up the horses that SBR has ready for adoption so that this organization can continue making a difference in the lives of the horses, and touching the lives of the families that make up their adopting community.

It is the mission of Saddlebred Rescue, Inc. to educate the public on concerns facing the Saddleseat breeds and save the unwanted horses from slaughter and return them to useful, productive lives. Their goal is to make a difference by educating the public, our youth, the horse industry, and the animal protection network who is becoming more involved in the prevention of cruelty to horses, providing alternatives/services to the dealers and auction houses, and the rehabilitation and re-homing of rescues. None of the work that the rescue has done would be possible without the financial support of many individuals, equine clubs, horse shows, equine youth groups, and a host of volunteers. The Global Federation of Animal Sanctuaries (GFAS), the only globally recognized organization providing standards for identifying legitimate animal sanctuaries, awarded Verified status to Saddlebred Rescue, Inc. as of August 1, 2012.

Saddlebred Summit Advances

Thursday, February 22, 2007

by Christy Howard Parsons

LEXINGTON, KY. - One of the major initiatives the American Saddlebred Horse Association undertook in 2006 was a **membership survey**, which truly amounted to a census, as every ASHA adult member was asked for their opinions. The purpose of the survey was to assess the current state of the breed and to aid the leadership in advancing the breed. Along with Dr. Steven Skinner and the University of Kentucky, ASHA formed focus groups to determine what questions to include on the survey.

In addition to overall questions asked of everyone, breeders, trainers, farriers, owners and veterinarians were asked to answer additional specific questions about their areas of knowledge.

While the full results of the survey have not been publicly released yet, the results have been studied by the Advancement Committee, and the challenges identified by the survey were discussed in an open forum with the membership.

The survey identified two chief issues as barriers to growth of the breed. Both **affordability and judging** were clearly issues to ASHA members according to the survey. It was also identified in the open comment portion of the survey that **some people thought the industry was unwelcoming to new people** or was considered elitist. While time ran short and members did not have much chance to respond to these issues in the open session on Saturday, Gayle Lampe did agree with the affordability issue and argued **that having fewer small horse shows where affordable horses can compete was a key issue.**

The survey also indicated that the perception of our judging was not as good as we would expect. Even isolating only actual judges' opinions still indicated a perceived problem in the subjective judging process.

Scott Matton summed up these perceptions by saying that he had spent many years in the beginning of his career experiencing bad judging. "But I've found that the better my horses get and the better my riders get, the better the judging gets."

Alan Balch suggested that perhaps ASHA should consider a peer review process that went a step beyond USEF's Licensed Officials rules. "We could be a leader in the subjectively judged disciplines," said Balch.

Art Zubrod encouraged ASHA members to be patient in making changes. "We do need entry level horses, entry level classes and entry level shows, but most of all we have to be supportive of these new people. I like some of the ideas we've heard, but it's going to take a long time to make these changes, seven or eight years perhaps, before we start seeing a difference."

Some of the changes Zubrod alluded to had been discussed in the earlier session on Friday. At that session, Balch released the facts and figures of the ASHA. While the financial report was very good in that expenses have continued to be cut and profits in 2006 approached $200,000, in the end the ASHA is a small organization with net assets (net of prize programs and including the building at cost) of only $1.1 million. This is quite small in terms of an ability to launch a major marketing initiative.

Balch reviewed some of the costs for television, radio, newspaper and outdoor billboard advertising. For example, KEEP, a Kentucky equine program spent over $1 million in nine weeks in only one state in advertising. "We are not in a position to spend money like this on advertising," explained Balch.

"But the most important assets we have to leverage are not our financial assets, but **our 8,800 member nationwide sales force.** If we could motivate our total database of people who love the American Saddlebred, even if they aren't an ASHA member, and arm them with a consistent message and repeat that same message relentlessly, then we can turn this ship around," said Balch.

"The web is absolutely the key, especially for the younger demographics we want to attract. This group understands network marketing, and we have to find a way to tap into this market," furthered Balch.

Balch also released 2006 data, although he cautioned that many of the figures cannot accurately be compared to prior years as stallion reports and registrations continue to come in after the year is over. **ASHA membership for 2006 was 8,627.** This number has continued to rise even after the large increase in 2004 due to a rule change requiring exhibitors at the World's Championship to be ASHA members.

Mares bred were 5,409 and stallion reporting were 921, but these numbers are certainly not final figures. However, it does appear these numbers are showing some decline, and "any decline is unacceptable," according to Balch. Registrations taken by year for any age horse were 2,860 in 2006, which shows a slight decline since 2001 when the number was 3,052, but these figures have been between 2,756 and 3,052 for the last seven years. Transfers taken by year for any age horse are also down. In 2006 there were 4,826 transfers compared to 5,376 in 2002. "Don't take this to mean I don't think we can do anything," said Balch. "There are lots of things we can do."

 **Ray Sheffield** before his death in **2007** had some **provocative comments** that he shared with this writer that are unpublished. He prepared these statements to be sent to an organization but he did not follow through. Sheffield was disturbed by the lack of interest in American Saddlebreds that is verified by many empty seats at horse shows. He remembered that in the early twentieth century that there was a Saddlebred columnist that kept the public and horse community informed.

"Today, the horse people do not get the coverage of their horses and farms that they once had. The exhibitors, trainers and riders need to be promoted as **celebrities** and **stars** to make people want to see the **competition** at horse shows. The contests have **action** that can only be described by discerning writers and perspicacious announcers. They can give color to the performance by critiquing the riders about their showmanship, style and physical abilities. The renowned Earl Teater was always looking behind him, knowing where all his competitors where situated. Look for something that stands out like old man Cordy Mountjoy who always wore a red tie. Remember Ben Wilson from Lawrenceburg who stood for many years barefooted at the entrance to the Kentucky State Fair gate. There he would be with a bushy gray beard, walking stick, and overalls with shoulder straps.

The newspaper writer must describe the event in such a way that it makes the reader want to see spirited competition. A professional announcer can make all the difference in giving some sparkle, interest and excitement to the event. His ability to describe the action that comes from the rider's command of the gaits creates interest. Outstanding riders have records of their own that need to be known. Any antics of their showmanship should be brought to the attention of the spectators. Anyone can show a horse but not everyone can perform with professional skills that make the horse excel. It should be mandatory that the announcer tell who are the horses, the owners and the riders. Announcers need to explain the professionalism of the judges and the protocol of judging.

It makes **Horse Sense**, let's call a horse show a horse **event**. Forget the showing, let's start **competing** because spectators want to see **action**. Yes, a Saddlebred is like poetry in motion…but let's tell them about it. It is time to use the expertise of the advertising directors of the big corporations of our Saddlebred owners. They can get together and be creative in planning campaigns of advertising for the Saddlebred. These promotional people could volunteer to meet several times a year at our horse events and access their programs. We need writers and reporters from the media to come and cover the horse event. They should give a build-up to draw people to the event. They should emphasize that horses are competing rather than showing and establish a friendly rivalry between horses. You can see dog shows, quarter horses and car races on television but no Saddlebreds.

Horse people should be **community** minded. Although we have special education programs for the handicapped in some areas, there is much more that can be done. In special education they have found that sometimes by just riding a horse the handicapped person can walk. The community needs to fall in love with the horse."

Ray Sheffield. the former publisher of The National Horseman, was known for his generosity. He gave advertising to trainers who were looking for a job; provided the ASHA, UPHA, American Saddlebred Museum and other organizations space gratis on a regular basis; and always cheerfully supported many horse shows with sponsorships.

Ray had a smile in his voice and a joke to tell. He was well known for his contagiously positive outlook on life. He also had a serious side, and had spent many hours, on more than one occasion, compiling statistics concerning the impact of the Kentucky State Fair and the Saddlebred industry in general upon the economy of the Commonwealth of Kentucky, which he presented to legislators.

Ray's spirits were buoyed when the American Saddlebred Horse Association honored him with its Meritorious Service Award on Feb. 19 at the 2005 ASHA annual meeting. The national organization told of his many decades of giving free advertising on a regular basis to numerous Saddlebred groups and various horsemen needing some help.

Though not a trainer or horse show exhibitor, Ray was a founding member of the American Saddlebred Pleasure Horse Association; received the 1982 ASHA Award of Merit,; named the 1984 UPHA Man of the Year and was inducted into the 1995 Kentucky State Fair Hall of Fame.

Mary Anne Cronan was elected to be President of ASHA in **2008**. She was one of "Helen Crabtree's equitation girls" who was the 1960 AHSA Saddle Seat Medal Final Champion and has become a leader in the Association. She was Chairwoman of the Kentucky State Fair Board, first time in the 63-year history of the Kentucky State Fair Board that a woman had been chosen for the position. Mary Anne has been Director of Kentucky Saddlebred Owners and Breeders Association, Kentucky Horse Park Foundation and United States Equestrian Federation. In 2004 she received the ASHA Meritorious Service Award and in 2010 the USEF Sportsmanship Award and Walter B Devereux Trophy was awarded.

Judy Werner returned with her servitude to the Presidency of ASHA in **2009-2011.** She has served as Vice President of Administration and Finance of the United States Equestrian Federation, Director of St. Louis National Charity Horse Show and Vice President of American Saddlebred Registry. Judy Werner has received numerous awards including: In 1998 her name was engraved on the Walter B. Devereux

Trophy as the recipient of the AHSA Sportsmanship Award; 1999 inducted to the Kentucky State Fair Hall of Fame; inducted to the St. Louis National Hall of Fame; 2002 recipient of the USA Equestrian Ellen Scripps Davis Memorial Breeders' Award; 2004 received the Lifetime Achievement Award from ASHA and 2013 received the Breeders Hall of Fame with her husband Roy.

For her years of service, she will be awarded the 2014 USEF Lifetime Achievement Award and will receive the Jimmy A. Williams Lifetime Achievement Trophy at the Pegasus Awards gala.

Redd Crabtree received the **2010 Lifetime Achievement Award**, the highest honor upon which one can be bestowed by ASHA because of his impact in the show ring by winning multiple World Championships and his willingness to be a volunteer in the American Saddlebred world. Redd is the son of the legendary Saddlebred trainers, Helen and Charles Crabtree who came to Shelby County, KY in 1958 from Rock Creek Riding Club in

Louisville, KY. Redd joined them in 1969 and they became one of the American Saddlebred industry's patriarch families and that's how they operated as a family. They were known as one of the greatest public training stable of its time. In one year alone, the stable had 58 horses

showing at the Kentucky State Fair.

There has been a parade of Saddlebred owners that have established their farms in Shelby County because of the influence of Redd Crabtree and his parents. Today, there are 91 American Saddlebred horse farms making Shelby County "The Saddlebred Capital of the World." This is compared with the early 1900's when there were only three prominent saddle horse show stables: Weissinger's Undulata Farm, J. C. Cook and Chas. L. Cook. Prior to this time period there was a trotting track in Shelbyville and trotting horses were more popular.

Iconic Redd Crabtree was approached by brothers, Edward "Hoppy" and R. H. Bennett, with their idea of having a first class Saddlebred Horse Show in Shelbyville. Redd and his wife Nancy were enthusiastic and with a coalition of local community leaders the horse show was launched in 1990. The UPHA elected Shelbyville their National Honor Show in 1993 and 1999.

Crabtree's contributions to the Saddlebred industry have been enduring and unselfish. He has been very steadfast about the American Saddlebred breed and its future and that it goes forward in the right direction, **that all the things our forefathers set forth in our Association, those ideals are upheld.**

Awards and Honors have been:

- President of American Saddlebred Grand National (ASGN) before it became part ASHA
- Founding member of United Professional Horsemen's Association (UPHA)
- Served as Vice President of UPHA - 1970, 1971 & 1972
- President of UPHA - 1973 & 1974
- President of American Saddle Horse Museum 1973-1975
- Inducted in 1993 Kentucky State Fair Hall of Fame
- Inducted in 1994 UPHA Hall of Fame
- Director and Vice President of American Saddlebred Horse Association (ASHA)
- Director of American Saddlebred Registry (ASR)
- Director of Kentucky Saddlebred Owners and Breeders Association (KSOA)
- Recipient of C. J. Cronan Sportsmanship Award in 1994 and in 2014
- First show horse trainer to be inducted in the Kentucky Athletic Hall of Fame.

American Saddlebred Horse Association

Executive Director **2010-2012**

Paula Johnson of Mound, MN, becomes the Executive Director of ASHA because of her strong leadership skills, a background with budgets, and excellent communication skills. Her experience includes working in very large corporate settings like Honeywell and Jostens, as well as other smaller companies. Johnson is a lifelong equine enthusiast who has bred and raised several breeds.

She had a short term with ASHA, but President Judy Werner said, "Her accomplishments are mainly unseen to the average member, but those of us who have worked with her and who know what the organization needed when she was hired, will be forever grateful to her. Paula made my life a lot easier as President and I wish her nothing but the best in her future endeavors."

Expansion of American Saddlebred Museum
Opened Apr. 9, 2010

"Showplace for Saddlebreds" is a 7,000 sq. ft. addition. The addition divides the museum into two wings—the John & Dorothy Lenore Gallery Wing and the Elisabeth M. Goth History Wing. The Gaylord Family Changing Exhibit Gallery houses the Museum's special exhibits; a George Ford Morris Art Gallery showcases the museum's Saddlebred collection by the noted artist. The History Wing has a newly renovated, state-of-the-art theater.

The ASB Museum houses the largest collection of Saddlebred artifacts in the world. The archives house trophies, photographs, tack, and artwork, including one of the most extensive collections of George Ford Morris Saddlebred artwork. The library houses over 2,500 volumes used by the members for bloodline and genealogical research. While the Museum serves as a resource to the Saddlebred industry, it also educates tens of thousands of visitors annually about the beauty, versatility and history of the American Saddlebred horse.

During **2010 Alltech FEI World Equestrian Games at the Kentucky Horse Park**, the ASB Museum had a special exhibit called **"This is the American Saddlebred,"** to display the versatility of today's American Saddlebred by showing it in all possible disciplines.

Tolley Graves, Executive Director, says, "The Museum's location at the Horse Park has positioned us to have access to every single visitor to WEG. Every person attending the games will walk past our building. This is an unparallele opportunity that we cannot afford to pass up." The actual attendance was 507,022 from over 60 countries. The Alltech FEI World Equestrian Games are the world championships of eight equestrian disciplines.

Museum Equine Art, Antique & Rare Book Auction

The annual auction was moved in **2011** from the "Round Barn" at The Red Mile to the Museum's new "Showplace for Saddlebreds" at the Kentucky Horse Park. It is held on Saturday during the Lexington Junior League Horse Show in July. Attendees can now enjoy the auction in the comfort of air conditioning! The Round Barn had been a very picturesque setting for the auction, but bidders, artwork and food were all at the mercy of the elements there. The auction has earned its reputation as a venue at which a variety of serious equine artwork, antiques, collectibles, rare books and historic artifacts can be purchased. Gross sales were over $113,000 in 2013, bringing total gross sales for all nine previous auctions to $1,474,123.

The **ASHA High Point Awards Program** was initiated in **2011** after considerable thought and effort by the Charter Club Council, comprised of volunteers from across the country who represent a broad spectrum of equestrian disciplines.

The High Point Awards Program recognizes competition achievement by registered American Saddlebreds and Half-Saddlebreds in a wide range of categories and disciplines, at all levels, not only in the "traditional" Saddlebred show ring, but also in open breed competition (such as open English pleasure, etc.) and sport horse disciplines. The two highest placing horses owned by active ASHA members in each category are named High Point Champion and Reserve Champion. The program also awards High Point winners in ten regions and Europe. The specific categories awarded in each region vary depending on regional availability and participation.

In **2011** ASR introduced the **American Saddlebred Registry Sport Horse Incentive Program**. Eligible horses are purebred Saddlebreds registered with the American Saddlebred Registry (ASR), and half-Saddlebreds registered with the Half-Saddlebred Registry of America (HSRA). ASHA took over the role of the administrator of HSRA on July 15, 1996. The owner must be a current member in good standing of ASHA. Eligible all-breed disciplines are Dressage, Western Dressage, Hunters, Jumpers, Combined Driving, Pleasure Driving, Reining, Eventing, Endurance, Limited Distance and Competitive trail. These horses are eligible for $15,000 in prize money, based on their participation and performance. The incentive is designed to identify and reward owners of American Saddlebreds competing in the Sport Horse Disciplines.

In September 2011, The American Saddlebred Horse Association became a supporter of HORSES and HOPE, which is a partnership with the Kentucky First Lady and the Kentucky Cancer Program. A HORSES and HOPE Trail Ride was held at the Kentucky Horse Park to benefit the fight against breast cancer.. This event honors breast cancer survivors, to cancer awareness, and to provide breast cancer education and mammography screening to horse industry workers. The Pink Stable is a committee of Kentucky horse owners, riders, trainers, farm owners and jockeys that support the HORSES and HOPE initiative. **Misdee Wrigley Miller**, a member of the Pink Stable and ASHA, served as Ambassador of the HORSES and HOPE program when she took her Dutch Harness horses to compete in Europe in 2014. She shared the program's best practices and encouraged international participation.

Tandy Patrick, a distinguished lawyer with Greenbaum, Doll, MacDonald law firm in Louisville and Lexington became President of ASHA in 2012. She is a lifelong owner, breeder, and exhibitor of American Saddlebreds. Her busy schedule includes: Director, Kentucky Horse Park, 2004-2008; Kentucky Horse Park Commission, Chairperson 2005-2008; Director, World Games 2010 Foundation, Inc., Member of Executive Committee, 2005-2010; Interim Chair of Board, 2007; Director, Kentucky State Fair Board, Member-in-Charge Worlds Championship Horse Show, 2007; member of the United Professional Horsemen's Association; member of the Kentucky Saddlebred Owners and Breeders Association; member of the United States Equestrian Federation and Director of Kentucky Horse Council (KHC) in 2014.

American Saddlebred Registry   Registrar **2012 -**

At the Feb. 20, **2010** ASR Board of Directors Meeting it was decided to create a Registrar position separate from the Association's Executive Secretary and reporting to the President of the Registry. The recommendation was accepted by the ASHA Board on May 1, 2012. **Lisa Duncan** accepted the offer of the position of Registrar commencing on June 25, 2012.

The Registrar's primary role is to manage and supervise the operation and affairs of the Registry, and administer the overall missions of the Registry, which are to establish, maintain and publish a register for the recording of pedigrees and transfers of ownership, and to guard the purity of the breed.

The ASHA Board said that **Lisa Duncan's** background and experience makes her uniquely qualified for this important position. Lisa is a lifelong horsewoman and is very knowledgeable about the breed. As a graduate of the University of Kentucky where she majored in Agriculture Education with a specialty in Equine Science, Lisa has over 20 years of experience working in various positions in the Saddlebred industry. Effective June 23, 2014, Lisa assumed the duties of Interim Executive Director for the ASHA on a temporary basis.

The ASR Board established a new mission statement: **The American Saddlebred Registry shall guarantee the purity of the breed through the establishment, maintenance and publication of an accurate register for the recording of pedigrees and the transfers of ownership of the American Saddlebred Horse. The Registry shall, in addition, administer the recognition and prize programs associated with the breed.**

 **Jimmy Robertson** started a **New Beginning in Saddlebred Auction Sales** on April 15, **2012** with phenomenal results. His Robertson Equine Sales opened at the Shelby County Fairgrounds, Shelbyville, KY, "The Saddlebred Capital of the World." Robertson offered an easily accessible web site containing photos and videos or a printed catalog containing smart phone friendly QR codes so viewers can quickly link to online video content of the consignment.

Phone bids were accepted and the sales were Webcast by Richfield Video Productions. A benchmark was set at the 2014 Spring Sale with a test run of RESnetSM, a custom database system that permits entries, hip numbers, barn and stall assignments, necessary paperwork, complete invoicing and more to be handled in a Web cloud-based secure environment. The Robertson's were using smart phones and tablets in the sales lane that enabled instant access up-to-minute statistics and information at any point during the auction.

These **technological advances** has given Jimmy Robertson a cutting edge in Saddlebred auction sales bringing consignors from across the country and buyers as far away as Canada. Jimmy was wise in hiring former Tattersalls personnel after it closed in 2011 with 117 years of operation. Another novel idea by Robertson is to offer a bonus prize money program as an added benefit to selected horse shows and purchasers of horses at one of his sales. "Helen and I believe in supporting and preserving horse shows and providing incentives for owners and exhibitors to participate," said Robertson.

Jimmy and his wife Helen, own and operate Infinity Stables, Simpsonville, KY. Helen balances her role has instructor and trainer. With numerous world's championship and national championship titles to the stable's credit, they are committed to the development and success of each Saddlebred.

Helen Robertson is the creator of the **UPHA Ribbons of Service** (ROS) program which began in 2009, allows young equitation riders to participate in horse show competitions while raising

funds for children with life-threatening illnesses. Robertson's founding vision was to motivate oftentimes-privileged children in the equestrian world to recognize and help seriously ill children who are fighting for their lives. ROS is operated under the banner of the UPHA with Robertson as the Chairwoman. Young equestrians must also commit to helping others through hours of tracked and verified hands-on community service. In 2013,

more than 30 participants raised $98,817 with $71,000 earmarked for St. Jude Children's Research Hospital.

Jimmy Robertson's service record is notable:

- President of United Professional Horseman's Association (UPHA) in 1990-91 and 2002-03
- Director of American Saddlebred Horse Association (ASHA) 2007-2010
- Treasurer of American Saddlebred Registry (ASR) 2010

Outstanding Awards have been:

- UPHA Richard E. Lavery Professional Horseman's Award
- UPHA Helen Crabtree Equitation Instructor of the Year Award in 1997
- ASHA C. J. Cronan Sportsmanship Award in 2000
- Kentucky State Fair Hall of Fame in 2007
- UPHA Chapter Horsemen of the Year in 2010
- ASHA Meritorious Service Award in 2012.

| Jimmy and Helen Robertson presented in 2010 | | Shirley Parkinson Professional Achievement Award |

Jimmy Robertson is the son of legendary Hall Of Famer Jim B. Robertson. His experience in the equine auction business began with his brother Walt; they helped their father when he conducted a Saddlebred Sale at least once a year for twenty years at the Jim B. Robertson Farm, Lexington, KY. Walt is a world famous equine auctioneer and has assisted Jimmy at Robertson Equine Sales.

Preceding Robertson Equine Sales in Kentucky was TSE/Tattersalls, Lexington, KY, famed as the oldest light horse market; known as "America's Most Famous Horse Mart" and affectingly called "Teater Town." The demise of TSE/Tattersalls came about when the owners of the property brought in construction experts to review the costs of upgrading the facility. When upgrades were estimated to be close to $1 million, the owners decided it made more sense to sell the property to a developer for a major student housing project. After 25 years of operation by Teater Saddlebred Enterprises, Inc., owners Ed and Suzie Teater announced their retirement.

 Young **Edward M. Teater** rode his spotted pony Steppin Fetchet at the Tattersalls Sale not knowing that someday he would be President of Teater Saddlebred Enterprises and conducting the sales at Tattersalls. When famous auctioneer, George Swinebroad, brought the hammer down on the last bid, it was for $1,000. "Ed" was fifteen years old when Mr. F. H. Eddy, Sec'y/Treas. of Tattersalls, and one of the most popular executives in the horse world; asked "Ed" if he would like to run the refreshment stand at the Tattersalls Sale. Ed accepted the offer and at 6:00 a.m. on the morning of the sale, he got his hamburgers, hot dogs, all the fixing's, soft drinks and coffee together for a big day. At 6:00 p.m. when "Ed" counted up his profit, he had $125, real well for a teenage boy's day of shrewd work.

This ingenuity continued with his wife, Suzie, at his side as his personal secretary and a library science background, they **started making improvements in the catalog and the handling of the horses that resulted in a steady increase in good, clean sales.** At the time the Teaters entered the auction business, quality horses selling at auction were few and far between barring infrequent dispersals. Ed Teater through hard work was able to transform Tattersalls into a legitimate, well-respected auction market for all caliber of horses on which the Saddlebred industry could rely. Having a formidable staff, Tattersalls handled record-breaking dispersal and consignment sales.

Ed is the son of Earl Teater who trained and showed the incomparable CHWing Commander in addition to a legion of well known World Champions; and nephew to Lloyd and Jay Teater who were luminaries of the horse show scene for many years. Ed had a successful career as a Saddlebred trainer beginning with Rock Creek Riding Club in Louisville, Dodge Stables (Castleton Farm), and North Ridge Farm owned by the Grove family in Minnesota.

Ed Teater's profile includes: ASHA C.J. Cronan Sportsmanship Award in 1988; Director of ASHA 1968-1987; Director of ASHA 1989-1997; Vice-President ASHA 1992- 1997; inducted into Kentucky State Fair Hall of Fame in 1997 and inducted into UPHA Tom Moore Hall Of Fame in 2001.

Mary Gaylord McClean   Elisabeth Goth

Mary Gaylord McClean and **Elisabeth Goth,** two distinguished Saddlebred Ladies known for the many championships they have won and should be recognized for their philanthropy. Each have served and given financially to the betterment of the Saddlebred industry.

Mary Gaylord supports Marion Therapeutic Riding Association (MTRA) that uses horseback riding to help physically and mentally challenged people build self-esteem and independence; she has been generous in her donation to UPHA Ribbons of Service Program that allows young equitation riders to participate in horse show competitions while raising funds for children with life-threatening illnesses.

Mary Gaylord is a contributor to Team American Saddlebreds, Inc. (TAS) whose mission is to assist American Saddlebreds that are in need, at risk of neglect or face a threat of slaughter. She contributes to UPHA Exceptional Challenge Cup Championship designed to give mentally and physically challenged riders the chance to compete and earn awards at a national level and Saddlebred Rescue, Inc. that adopts Saddlebreds, Hackneys and Morgans from situations that have placed them in danger. She was a major contributor to Shelby County Fairgrounds.

Elisabeth Goth is the "Gold Level Sponsor" of the prestigious NHS "Good Hands" Finals that are held at the Mid-America Mane Horse Show, Springfield, IL. and Elisabeth donated $1,000 college scholarship to one of the top riders. Elisabeth is a contributor to Team American Saddlebreds, Inc. (TAS) whose mission is to assist American Saddlebreds that are in need, at risk of neglect or face a threat of slaughter.

The 2007 ASHA Junior Exhibitor Driving Challenge was funded by Elisabeth Goth at the American Royal, Kansas City, MO. It was developed to promote the American Saddlebred driving divisions among junior exhibitors. In 2013 she was host to an "Afternoon Fiesta" at the Lexington Junior League Horse Show that featured many special guests speaking of how they transitioned from the junior exhibitor ranks to young adulthood, while still staying involved in the American Saddlebred industry. In 2014 Elisabeth was host to a Hawaiian Luau at the Lexington Junior League Horse Show.

The **ASHA Lurline Roth Sportmanship Award** was presented in 1990 to Mary Gaylord and to Elisabeth in 2000. The **ASHA Breeder of the Year Award** was given to Mary Gaylord in 2009 and to Elisabeth in 2012. Both received the **UPHA Sallie B. Wheeler Distinguished Service Award.**

Mary Gaylord McClean was awarded the 2002 USA Equestrian Bill Robinson Trophy. She was President of AHHS and served on the Board of Directors. In 2005 she was a Director of KSOBA. Mary Gaylord was inducted into Kentucky State Fair Hall of Fame in 2003. In 2010 she was inducted into the American Road Horse and Pony Association Hall of Fame. In 2012 she received the UPHA Alvin C. Ruxer Lifetime Commitment Award.

Elisabeth Goth was the winner of the 1997 AHSA/Hertz Equestrian of the Year Award. She served on the ASHA Board of Directors from 1998-2004 and has been elected to serve in 2015. She has been a Board member of the National Horse Show and the California Saddle Horse Breeders' Association. She currently represents ASHA on the USEF Board of Directors. In 2014 she was Secretary of the American Saddlebred Museum.

ASHA participates in the **Kids Barn** at the Kentucky Horse Park that is a fun and educational stop. Each stall in the Kids Barn features different interactive exhibits, ranging from veterinarian and general equine info and nutrition to different competitive disciplines. The Saddlebred stall is one of 20 stalls designed to engage school-age children in discovering the wonder of horses.

Open in **May 2012** the Saddlebred stall has a cutback saddle for children to sit on. Another stall has popular horse books. One has a buggy kids can pretend to drive and another has saddles on barrels that kids can pretend to ride. The Kids Barn also features live horse demonstrations, giving children a chance to touch and even help groom horses.

Scott Matton, President of ASR in **2012**, and his wife Carol own Knollwood Farm, Hartland, WI. In 1983 he was Horse Person Of The Year, American Saddlebred Association of Wisconsin; 2001 received the ASHA Meritorious Service Award; 2004 Scott and Carol were recipients of the UPHA Helen Crabtree Instructor of the Year award and in 2005 they were honored with The National Horseman's prestigious Castleman Award for excellence in the industry.

Scott is **outspoken in his support for the American Saddlebred industry and its future being largely dependent upon Lesson/Academy programs. Lesson Programs** teach the valuable lessons of equitation and horsemanship, along with the joy and appreciation of interacting with a horse. Lesson programs are designed for riders at all levels who may or may not own their own horse or pony. Some lesson programs have a double saddle that allows the instructor to ride with the child so that she/he can accomplish more each lesson. The most important thing in a lesson program is that it's fun, it's safe, and that the rider always learning and being challenged.

The American Saddlebred Horse Association **Academy Awards program** encourages and recognizes juveniles and adults participating in academy classes at horse shows throughout the country. Academy classes create an opportunity for beginning saddle seat riders to develop and fine-tune their horsemanship skills, sportsmanship, and appreciation for the American Saddlebred.

An Academy class is any class offered at a local tournament in which two or more stables are participating, or any class at an open show that is designated "academy." Participants compete on horses designated as school horses, or horses that are regularly used in riding lesson program instruction. Acceptable riding attire is jodhpurs or dark pants, boots and dress shirt or a sweatshirt bearing the stable's logo. Riding suits are unacceptable, and hard hats are optional.

National Academy Championship Horse Show was created by ASHA member, **Joyce Webster** of B & W Stables, Hartselle, AL. It is the largest, most prestigious academy horse show in the country held at the Miller Arena, Murfreesboro, TN. All proceeds are given to St. Jude's Children Hospital to help children with life threatening disease.

This is a show where top academy riders from all over the nation come together in the spirit of competition. Every rider must qualify in a preliminary class in order to compete for a Championship class. The top 10 ribbon winners from each age group will move on to the Championship rounds. In **2013** there were 769 entries from 16 states and the proceeds were $25,000 to St. Jude's Children Hospital.

Gayle Lampe, Life Member of ASHA and Professor Emeritus, Equestrian Science - Saddle Seat at William Woods University, Fulton, MO. She has been an instrumental force in the development of the country's first four-year academic degree program in equestrian science that is nationally acclaimed and **sets a standard for College/University equine studies**.

When she leaves her busy teaching schedule, she demonstrates her expertise in horsemanship:

- Winning in 2003 the Ladies Five-Gaited Championship at the Kentucky State Fair on Callaway's Born to Win.
- Won the Ladies Five-Gaited Championship at the UPHA American Royal National Championship Horse show in 2003, 2005, 2007, 2008 and 2009 on Born to Win.
- Won the World Champion Ladies Five-Gaited gelding title in 2009, with Born to Win.

    Among her many honors are:
    - 1995 UPHA Equitation Instructor of the Year Award
    - 2004 ASHA Lurline Roth Sportsmanship Award
    - 2007 World's Championship Horse Show at the Kentucky State Fair, Audrey Gutridge Award
    - 2007 General John B. Castleman Award.

American Saddlebred Horse
Association

Executive Director **2012 -2014**

Karen Winn started as Executive Director of ASHA in **July 2012**. She comes from the United States Pony Club, where she served over 14 years and recently as Chief Operating Officer. Prior to her tenure at the Pony Club, Karen served as the Business Manager for the American Hanoverian Society for 5 years.

Karen has a Bachelor of Science in Animal Science with concentration in Equine Science from the University of Massachusetts, and a Bachelor of Science in Accounting from the University of Kentucky. She is a Certified Sports Marketing Professional, a licensed USEF "R" judge in dressage and eventing, and an FEI Eventing Judge and Chief Steward.

"In this exciting time of new ideas, new directions and exciting initiatives at ASHA, Karen's unique combination of skills and experience makes her uniquely qualified to serve as the new

CEO for ASHA," said ASHA President Tandy Patrick. After several years of service to the organization, Karen Winn resigned effective June 20, 2014.

The Association Board of Directors met on **July 10, 2012** and the Publications Committee reported that the American Saddlebred magazine was out of date and it is very difficult for the magazine to succeed in today's very competitive and changing media environment. The Board unanimously voted to suspend publication of the magazine.

However, the Association announced that it would produce a hardbound book known as the **"Journal of the American Saddlebred"** that will be distributed free to its members starting in the winter issue of 2014 with invaluable breeding statistics and focus on the bloodstock of our industry, the Journal will feature historic articles.

At the Association Board meeting on Feb 13 & 15, 2014, **Randy Cates**, Chairman of Publications Committee, proposed and it was agreed to have a printed version of the three eZines (email magazines) in 2014 for members who have paid an additional $20. These publications would be **"Special Editions"** that could be utilized as a promotional tool, to include educational and historical articles, include human interest stories, articles on youth/Charter Clubs, and be 'public-oriented'.

A new Mission Statement was introduced: **The mission of the American Saddlebred Horse Association is to promote, improve and protect the grace, intelligence and versatility of the American Saddlebred, and to provide programs and services supporting our members, while fostering public awareness of the breed.**

Online voting begins December 19, 2012

To elect directors of the American Saddlebred Horse Association
This online ballot is to be used to elect six (6) Directors to the Board of Directors of the American Saddlebred Horse Association, each for a three-year term beginning in 2013 and ending in 2016.

ASR introduced the **Mare Harmony Program** in **2013**. The new program will help stimulate breeding by providing a venue to advertise American Saddlebred mares for lease. In addition, Mare Harmony offers the option to purchase embryo(s) / oocyte (s) from advertised mares. The mares are listed on the ASHA web site.

The ASHA and UPHA have announced that both organizations are in support of the **'Prevent All Soring Tactics Act of 2013'** proposed federal legislation that was introduced in **April 2013** and has been referred to the House Committee on Energy and Commerce. This legislation is intended to strengthen the Horse Protection Act, by increasing fees and penalties for the soring of horses. "ASHA President, Tandy Patrick, added that "the ASHA is opposed to any inhumane treatment of horses, including soring".

Soring is an abusive practice used by some horse trainers in the Tennessee Walking Horse, Spotted Saddle Horse, and Racking Horse industry. It usually involves the use of action devices, chemicals, pads, wedges or other practices to cause pain in the horse's forelegs and produce an accentuated show gait for competition. Despite the existence of a federal ban on soring for over forty years, this cruel practice continues in some segments of the walking horse industry.

The **Amateur Owner Trainer** classes are a program promoted and established by the ASHA Charter Club Council. **Betsy Boone** of Concord, NC made this recommendation to the Council and now it is a reality. These classes are for the owner who trains his/her own horses and wants classes to show his/her horses without the pressure of showing against professionally trained horses. The ASHA and UPHA have teamed up to produce an Amateur Owner Trainer (AOT) Reference List. This directory includes one to three UPHA members in each chapter who are willing to help an Amateur Owner Trainer in their area. To volunteer to be on the list is free, but the advice does not need to be, charges for services rendered are up to each individual on the list. The support a professional would give an AOT could range from a training tip, to helping to look for a horse to purchase, aiding in selling a horse, giving a lesson or two, or even allowing AOTs to stable at the end of their aisle at horse shows.

Youth Conference

2013 ASHA Youth Field trip

One of the most successful achievements is the youth movement by ASHA. Shown are the increased number of youth that attended the **2013** conference and participated in a field trip that took them to Shelbyville and Louisville. The first stop was at Undulata Farm, owned by Edward

"Hoppy" Bennett, where they toured the mansion and got to see work outs by Undulata's Thriller, 2012 Two-Year-Old Five-Gaited Reserve World's Champion, Crystal Pistol, and Undulata's Ginni. "Hoppy" explained to them how Shelbyville came to be known as the "American Saddlebred Capital of the World".

The next stop was to Claudia Sanders Dinner House for the ASHA Youth Awards Luncheon. The buses were loaded again and headed to Louisville Equestrian Center where Betsy Webb and her drill team welcomed them with an exhibition and then a tour of the barn. The last stop on the tour was the Rock Creek Riding Club, where they were greeted by Moe Anson and Chad Cole. Moe pointed out pictures adorning the walls and gave them an interesting history about the Rock Creek Riding Club. Brenda Newell, ASHA Senior Programs Administrator, has worked tirelessly for years to put the youth movement forward with the current help of Germaine Johnson, Chair of ASHA Youth Committee.

Faithful Friends Wall of Honor campaign was launched by ASHA in **2013** where you may honor your favorite horse with sponsorship of a name plate to be featured on the ASHA website. There is a tax deductible donation of $200 to ASHA towards a technology upgrade, which will enhance the ASHA website and help support the advancement of our American Saddlebreds. Write a story about your special American Saddlebred and photos are welcomed.

Heartfelt expressions have been posted such as: "holler her name, and she'd come running, whinnying loudly all the way - excitedly nickers whenever he hears my voice in the barn, always ready for a peppermint and hug - the second she heard my voice, she would start nickering and she wouldn't stop until I opened her door to pet her - He was the kindest horse I've ever known... completely safe around tots and elders - In honor of the most intelligent, kind, gentle, beautiful companion a person could have for 20 years - that rare combination of beauty, talent and incredible patience and good sense. He was truly a once in a lifetime horse!"

State of Affairs: "The Future of the Professional Horse Trainer" was a presentation given at the United Professional Horsemen's Convention on **Jan. 17, 2014**. The allegation from the findings of Saddlebred trainers, Jim and Jenny Taylor of Memory Lane Farm, Medina, OH, along with Todd Graham of Royal Winds Farm, Ona, WV; the future of our great show horses, and the future of everyone who has chosen them as their livelihood, is at stake.

Based on a 52% drop in the foal crop from 2006 – 2012 and an alarming drop of breeding stallions; from 2006 - 2012 the number of Stallion Service Reports received by the American Saddlebred Registry has dropped 47%. It was found that 45% of the horses shown in eight top horse shows were 10 years old or older and would need to be replaced since they are nearing retirement or an alternate career.

Assumptions were made that indicated in 11 years each of the 600 UPHA trainers will have only 10 horses in training. If 300 of the UPHA trainers each have 20 horses in training, the remaining

300 will need to seek a new career!!!

Allie Layos, Editor-at-Large, *Saddle & Bridle* magazine, in her **Jan. 27, 2014** article, "To rescue an industry: where do we go from here" had some salient facts. "**The problem, put simply, is this: breeding numbers are down because there is nowhere to place the horses. There is nowhere to place the horses because the industry is getting smaller and smaller. The industry is getting smaller and smaller because there is no way for normal, average people to participate in it.**

"Let's be honest – at most shows, what are they going to see? Two brown horses going around in a circle doing basically the same thing over and over, with no explanation as to what is happening. **What else does the average horse show consist of today? An audience made up of the friends and immediate families of the exhibitors.**

"**Normal families can't spend $100,000 on their child's chosen sport.** True, not all Saddlebreds are equally expensive. But one has to remember that even a $10,000 horse is far more expensive than a lacrosse stick and the **upkeep of a "cheap" horse is the same as an expensive one**; cheap horses still eat, still need training, and still need to see farriers and vets regularly. Cheap horses don't cost less to show, either – and the trailering bills and entry fees aren't any less costly because the horse was cheap.

"**The end result is simply this: we are pricing out the average person.** If we want to grow our industry – **have a reason to breed more horses** – we need to get people there to see our horses. First, we need to stop catering solely to ourselves and **start devoting more time and energy to creating an event worth attending.** Look at the successful models, the handful of shows that do draw crowds. What do they offer that most don't? **Food, fairs, exhibitions, pamphlets and explanations of what is happening in the ring**.

"**I can't tell you how many times I've spoken with an area local who had no idea that a horse show was taking place in their own city.** Put a tip in to the local media. Put a sign out on the main road. Both are simple and free or inexpensive. Once we get the people there, we need to make them feel welcome. When people do want to get involved, **academy programs are a good start**; some barns have had major success starting academy riders and eventually moving them up to the performance divisions with their own horses.

"Lastly, **don't overprice your horses. Everybody wants a cut of the commission** and everybody wants to make up the money they've sunk into the training and upkeep of a horse, but is your 2-year-old that has never shown really worth $100,000? There is no easy fix, but we have a great product called the American Saddlebred, and if ever there was something worth fighting for, I think we'd all agree that this is it."

May the case rest upon the owners, trainers and horse show managers to be resolved.

**"Where Have All the Horses Gone"?** This was the topic at the American Horse Council National Issues Forum on **June 24, 2014.**" Leaders from breed registries, racing, showing, the various disciplines, veterinarians and other stakeholders spoke about the decline in registered horses and the impact on their segment of the horse industry including American Saddlebreds.

There was no one reason given by the various speakers for the drop in registered horses. The economy was cited as the single largest factor. **Tim Capps**, Director of the Equine Industry Program at the University of Louisville believes the horse industry was in a bubble that peaked around 2004, which was similar to an earlier bubble in the 1980s, that exacerbated the situation. The increasing cost of horse ownership and participation in shows; concerns about welfare; and increased competition for leisure and gambling dollars were all also cited as playing a roll. The forum clearly identified the problem is not only a decline in the number of registered horses, but also a decline in horse owners and people participating in horse activities.

Jane Simmons writing in her Word Portrait column in **September 2014** issue of Saddle & Bridle magazine about the horse population makes these statements, "The prevailing reasons given to me for why this so-few-horses environment exist today in the show horse world is summed up basically in three key words: **money**, **urbanization**, and **estrangement**."

"In the heyday of the last century, hundreds and hundreds of families throughout the country attended horse shows, either showing horses of their own or going to see friends' horses compete. Thus, county fairs and small town horse shows kept many horse lovers busy nearly half the year, and definitely every weekend during a summer. These fun events did not cost a lot of money.

In the decades of the 20th Century, more people lived on acreage, and entertainment choices were fewer, more down-home, and less hi-tech. Today, in the 21st Century, people are estranged from this close association with a life style populated by horses.

Gayle Lampe, Adjunct Professor of Equestrian Science at William Woods University in Fulton, Missouri, said the answer to this "grave situation" is to "develop more riding lesson programs for the saddle seat type of riding" to encourage more people's interest. "If people were buying, breeders would be breeding" the horses necessary to fulfill "the law of supply and demand." Gayle pointed out she was not talking "breed specific, but rather seat specific."

ASR statistics indicate in 2012, registrations were down about 3% from 2011; transfers were down about 1.6%; foal crop registration was up by 6.7%. In 2013, registrations were down 15% from 2012, transfers were down 13% and foals registrations were down 27%. The total registrations processed (includes all foaling years) in 2013 were 1,536. This total includes 1,017 for 2013 foals that were registered in 2013. It must be noted that this is not the first such decline in the number of horses and in previous instances there was later a rebound in numbers and the horse industry often parallels the wider economy which the current situation closely mirrors.

Photo by Howie Schatzberg

Inaugural exhibitors and trainers welcomed to **2014** KY State Fair. Each is given a special ribbon and a souvenir gift bag.

Randy Cates, ASHA Board member had the vision to establish this popular event three years ago. He said, "We feel that it is important to recognize first-timers to Louisville, to let them know how glad we are that they are here; it is gratifying to see the first-timer ribbons proudly displayed at the barns throughout the week."

- Eventing

- Dressage

- Companionship

- Show Ring

- Western

- Driving

Versatility Is Recognized

American Saddlebred Versatility Association (VERSA) is a newly recognized Charter Club for **2014** by ASHA. VERSA is a non-profit corporation incorporated in the state of Missouri. It was founded in 2012 to promote the versatile character and use of the American Saddlebred and Half-Saddlebred horses, and to educate the public. In addition it aims to help riders and drivers of any particular discipline to connect with others in their same discipline.

The VERSA group seeks to dispel the myth that American Saddlebreds are "designer horses", suitable only for animated, showy classes at big horse shows, for those who can afford to show on a national level. It seeks to showcase the breed in as many Equestrian disciplines as possible, demonstrating the wide range of activities they are well suited for. Today it isn't uncommon to see Saddlebreds not only performing in the show ring in performance (English and Western), Equitation and driving classes, but also performing at successfully high levels in Hunter and Dressage classes, in Eventing competitions. It is also not uncommon to see these horses being trail ridden and kept at home as a family friendly backyard horse. VERSA's additional focus is on the Saddlebred owner who simply wants to enjoy the breed and all the activities they can so aptly participate in, even though they themselves may not actually participate in all areas. A common misconception has prevented many people from becoming involved in the American Saddlebred breed since they are perceived only as show horses that require professional training. Once people get to know an American Saddlebred, they come to understand the horse's versatility, and, even more important, the enjoyment and companionship that this breed brings to their owners.

The dedication of the ASHA and a number of enthusiasts to finding good homes and "jobs" for all Saddlebreds has led to the development of the American Saddlebred Sport Horse division. . In fact, the American Saddlebred Sport Horse Association (ASBSA) was formed specifically for the purpose of "educating both the sport horse buying public and the American Saddlebred breeders, owners and trainers about the viability of the American Saddlebred as a premier sport horse."

The Saddlebred is perhaps best known for competing in the "traditional" disciplines of saddle seat, including five-gaited, three-gaited, park, show pleasure, country pleasure and equitation, as well as in the show driving disciplines such as fine harness, along with show pleasure and country pleasure driving. The development of the Western pleasure division has led to substantial competition for the Saddlebred in Western tack. Horses now compete in Western pleasure, Western country pleasure and working Western pleasure, offering even more competitive opportunities for the Saddlebred to demonstrate the versatility for which it is so well known.

Sport horses compete in a number of disciplines, including dressage, eventing, hunter, hunter paces, jumpers, sport horse in-hand, combined driving, trail riding, competitive and endurance riding, pleasure driving, barrel racing, reining and side saddle. In an effort to continue promotion of the breed for use in these disciplines, both the ASHA and the ASBSA operate recognition programs for sport horses. It would be fair to say that the best reason for anyone to want to own a Saddlebred is their exceptional versatility. The expanding use of the American Saddlebred in both its traditional and more non-traditional disciplines makes it highly marketable. **It is**

certainly this versatility that secures the future of the breed.

On the morning of February 14, **2014** during the ASHA Annual Convention and Youth Conference, Allen Bosworth, Chief Operating Officer of Erwin Penland Advertising and Chair of the ASHA's Marketing Committee, unveiled a new and exciting marketing plan and **logo** for ASHA.

The **new marketing plan** includes implementation of programs and initiatives to achieve the following goals: 1. Increase memberships in ASHA, 2. Increase the registration of American Saddlebred Foals, 3. Increase the number of American Saddlebred Lesson Programs & Riding Instructors and the use of American Saddlebreds as lesson horses in every discipline and the knowledge of Saddle Seat as a whole and 4. Effectively position the American Saddlebred so that it consistently represent the breed to key audiences.

Along with the strategic implementation of the aforementioned goals, the ASHA has unveiled a new logo which was approved by the ASHA Board of Directors in January, and the slogan, "America's Spirited Beauty"… ASB.

R. H. Bennett was awarded the **2014** ASHA Wing Commander Medal. The criteria for winning this honor is the demonstration of outstanding service to ASHA and the breed. His primary focus has been to expand the popularity of the American Saddlebred Horse through the production and distribution of video. R. H. founded Richfield Video productions in 1982 and started live webcasting of American Saddlebred horse shows

throughout the country in 2009. This medium gives the opportunity for American Saddlebred enthusiasts to see many horse shows in their own home.

Bennett is the co-founder and manager of the Shelbyville Horse Show, Shelbyville, KY since 1990 and has been manager of the Shelby County Fair Horse Show since 1995. He received the Herman R. Miles Horse Show Manager of the Year award in 1993 and 2003.

Futurities in **2014** remain a mainstay of ASR. The first Futurity was in 1927 and is now known as the ASR Kentucky Futurity. Another Futurity that has been added is the ASR Kentucky Amateur Futurity that is a sequel to the first except all entries are to be shown in the ring by amateurs only. The National Three-Year-Old Futurity allows an entry to choose one class from Five-Gaited, Three-Gaited, Fine Harness Three-Gaited Park and Three-Gaited Park Pleasure.

William D. Wise (Bill) has been given credit as creator of the **American Saddlebred Registry Sweepstakes.** The program is designed to perpetuate the breeding, training and showing of the American Saddlebred horse. They are a great benefit in promoting the breed and bringing new people into the industry. Entries in the Three-and Four-Year-Old Sweepstakes compete in the following classes: Three-Gaited, Five-Gaited, Fine Harness and Three-Gaited Park Pleasure. Entries in the Two-Year-Old Sweepstakes will compete in the following classes: Three-Gaited Park and Fine Harness. Since its inception, the ASR Sweepstakes has awarded more than $5 million in prize money through **2013**.
Honors received by "Bill" are:

- Named the United Professional Horsemen's Association horseman of the year in 1981
- Horseman of the year by the American Saddlebred Horse Association in 1983
- Inducted into the UPHA Hall of Fame in 2004
- Inducted in Kentucky State Fair Hall of Fame in 2009
- Received Wing Commander Medal in 2009
- Inducted into the Mercer County Fair & Horse Show Hall of Fame in 2014.

American Saddlebred Select strives to acknowledge and honor the achievements of registered American Saddlebred horses in all recognized competitive events. Points are earned at competitions approved by an organization regarded as the national or international sanctioning group for that equine activity in divisions recognized by that organization. Horses enrolled in the program earn points toward three levels of achievement: bronze, silver and gold. There are four different sections of competition where points may be accrued include, dressage, eventing, carriage/combined driving and endurance/competitive trail riding. American Saddlebred Select winners are regularly honored in the American Saddlebred Reference Directory, and each level of achievement is distinguished with a certificate and noted in the horse's permanent ASR file.

United States Equestrian Federation [USEF] serves as the National Governing Body for Equestrian Sport. The primary objective is to uphold the welfare of horses, regardless of value, as a primary consideration in all activities. The United States Equestrian Federation requires that horses be treated with kindness, respect, and the compassion they deserve, and never be subjected to mistreatment.

Curator

Kim Skipton

Executive Director

Tolley Graves

2014 Museum Special Exhibit Team presenting **Oak Hill Farm - A Jewel of the Bluegrass**

American Saddlebred Museum's Showplace for Saddlebreds has six decades of incomparable success in the exhibit produced by Kim Skipton, Curator. The exhibit features the legacy of Oak Hill Farm and Jean McLean Davis. Oak Hill Farm is located in Harrodsburg, Kentucky and has long been synonymous with world's champion Saddlebreds and the tradition of excellence begun by owner Jean McLean Davis.

Featured in the exhibit are hundreds of items and artifacts donated by Davis' estate. Included are trophies, ribbons, photographs, paintings, sculptures, and assorted memorabilia from Jean's personal collection. Videos play throughout the Museum with rarely seen photo footage of Jean and her horses from the 1940s through the early 1990s. This was a once in a lifetime chance to learn more about the woman and the horses of the legendary Oak Hill Farm.

Other **outstanding exhibits** in past years:

2000 - Wing Commander, Passing in review
2001 - A Century of Silver: The Trophies of the Kentucky State Fair World's Championship
     Horse Show
2002 – The Generals' Horse – "Saddlers" in the Civil War
2003 – Breaking the Mold: The American Saddlebred in Castings and Carvings
2004 – The Spindletop Legacy: Legends and Luminaries
2005 - The House of Bourbon: Bourbon County's Saddlebred Kingdom

2006 - A Treasure Trove of Saddlebred History – Past Treasures, Recent Acquisitions and the
       Stories Behind Them
2007 - Out of the Shadows: Bringing to Light Black Horsemen in Saddlebred History
2008 - For the Love of a Horse: Children and Saddlebreds
2009 - Moments of Merit: Select Pieces of Saddlebred History
2010 - This is the American Saddlebred
2011 - Celebrities: Saddlebreds and Personalities from the Silver Screen, Cinema and History
2012 - Where Were You in '62
2013 - The Art of Selling with Saddlebreds: The Show Horse in Vintage Advertising

American Saddlebred Horse
Association

Executive Director **2014 -**

Bill Whitley of Cary, NC was named Executive Director by the Board of Directors of the
American Saddlebred Horse Association (ASHA) in October 2014. Bill is well known and
highly regarded in the American Saddlebred industry. He has been an American Saddlebred
trainer and had a 33-year career with the North Carolina State Treasurer's Office, where he
managed a team of 10 employees and a $68 billion portfolio of investments. He has been
selected as Horse World's People's Choice Ringmaster for the past 16 years and has been show
manager for the North Carolina State Championship Charity Horse Show. Bill has been on the
ASHA Board of Directors and served as Treasurer.

"Bill Whitley is the ideal person to move the ASHA into the future," said ASHA President
Tandy Patrick. "In this exciting time of new ideas, new directions and exciting initiatives at
ASHA, Bill's unique combination of skills and experience coupled with his passion for and
knowledge of the American Saddlebred industry makes him uniquely qualified to serve as the
new Executive Director of the ASHA."

American Saddlebred Acronym/Abbreviations:

- AAC, All American Cup;
- AAHC, All American Horse Classic;
- AHHS, American Hackney Horse Society;
- AHSA, American Horse Shows Association

- ANHS, Alltech National Horse Show;
- ASAC, American Saddlebred Association of the Carolinas;
- ASB, American Saddlebred;
- ASB, American Spirited Beauty;
- ASBSA, American Saddlebred Sport Horse Association;
- ASGN, American Saddlebred Grand National ;
- ASHA, American Saddlebred Horse Association;
- ASHBA, American Saddlebred Horse Breeders Association;
- ASM, American Saddlebred Museum;
- ASPHA, American Saddlebred Pleasure Horse Association;
- ASR, American Saddlebred Registry;
- ATO, Amateur Trainer Owner;
- BHF, Broodmare Hall of Fame;
- CH, Champion;
- GFAS, Global Federation of Animal Sanctuaries;
- HSRA, Half-Saddlebred Registry of America;
- KHC, Kentucky Horse Council;
- MTRA, Marion Therapeutic Riding Association;
- ROS, Ribbons of Service;
- SBR, Saddlebred Rescue, Inc.;
- TAS, Team American Saddlebreds, Inc.;
- UPHA, United Professional Horsemen's Association;
- USAE, United States of America Equestrian;
- USEF, United States Equestrian Federation;
- VERSA, American Saddlebred Versatility Association;
- WEG, World Equestrian Games.

— ⚡ —

Commentary: It is with humble appreciation that I have this opportunity to compile and write about the contributions of American Saddlebred Visionaries. They are the "Movers and Shakers" and through their discernment and foresight have brought about explicit changes in ASHA, ASR, ASM and other entities.

The American Saddlebred horse was known as the **"Kentucky Saddler"** during the Civil War when used for mounts for such officers as General Robert E. Lee's "Traveller" of the Confederate Army, General Ulysses S. Grant's "Cincinnati" of the Union Army and Brigadier General John Hunt Morgan's "Gaines Denmark" (influential sire) of the Confederate Calvary.

The American Saddlebred horse is known as the **"peacock" of the show ring** and carries himself with an attitude that eludes description; some call it class, some call it style, but everyone agrees it is a presence.

Louis Taylor in his book *The Horse America Made,* 1944, explains how blood strains and careful breeding went to produce the American Saddlebred horse and it is truly **The Horse America Made**. One has only to admire their proud stance with heads held high and high stepping through their trademark five gaits to appreciate the appropriateness of the nicknames.

Today, is a new era when the American Saddlebred horse is recognized as the **"Versatility Horse."** The American Saddlebred is suited for a wide range of activities in many equestrian disciplines. Versatility is the footprint of the present and the future. There are viable suggestions made by several different writers in this treatise; I trust they will not fall on deaf ears. The American Saddlebred industry is in a crisis; there is both disillusionment and hope with Saddlebred enthusiasts.

I want to remember all the unsung heroes of the American Saddlebred industry. They are the committee members, the personnel working in the offices of the Saddlebred entities and the caretakers of the horses in the barns. Their dedication and devotion to their responsibilities have made it possible for the enjoyment and companionship that this breed brings to their owners and trainers.

There may be some notable members of the Saddlebred industry that this writer has overlooked; if so, I trust they will be recognized in the future.

THANK YOU! **To the Saddlebred Loyalists** who shared their wisdom in the development of this book. Answered Questionnaire: Judy Werner, Dr. Simon Fredericks, Keith D. Bartz and Jim Aikman; Critiqued Story: Judy Werner, Mary Anne Cronan, Charles J. "Mike" Cronan IV, Tolley Graves, Kim Skipton and Jim Aikman; Collateral Information: Scarlett Mattson and Mae Condon; Friends: Dr. Richard G. Edwards, Dr. Maurice G. Cook, Dr. Xavier Johan Webb, Richard B. Cook, Esq. and Billye N. Cook, Wife.

Acknowledgment: This history could not have been compiled and written without the inspiration and assistance of **Mae Condon**. Mae being a former owner of American Saddlebreds, a volunteer worker and staff employee of ASHA, and dedicated member of ASHA committees has shared her extraordinary experience and knowledge.

Author: Chas. L. Cook, Jr. son of American Saddlebred trainer, Charlie Cook, of 1908-1941, etc. Holding the silver cup and multiple colored ribbon received in 2003 when his father was inducted posthumously into Kentucky State Fair Hall of Fame. Father is recognized for *Jonquil*, World's Three-Gaited Grand Champion for four consecutive years 1926-1929 and trained 1922 World's Five-Gaited Grand Champion "*Easter Star*" and rode to Reserve World's Five-Gaited Grand Champion in 1921.

I had the pleasure of riding in pair classes with my father as a child at the 1936 Kentucky State Fair and showing saddle horses when my father was Manager of V. V. Cooke's Meadow View Farm in Louisville. After a business career, I have maintained an interest in the breed by writing about Saddlebred memories of the past.

Disclaimer: To the best of my ability, this compiler/writer has tried to be accurate in the history as written. I do not assume and hereby disclaim any liability to any party for any loss, damage, or disruption caused by errors or omissions, whether such errors or omissions result from negligence, accident, or any other cause.

CPSIA information can be obtained
at www.ICGtesting.com
Printed in the USA
LVHW051504190223
739888LV00014B/1209

9 781935 538097